108

W9-CBR-339

SCIENTIFIC
AMERICAN™
CUTTING-EDGE SCIENCE™

Mysteries of the Milky Way

ROSEN
PUBLISHING®

New York

Published in 2008 by The Rosen Publishing Group, Inc.
29 East 21st Street, New York, NY 10010

The articles in this book first appeared in the pages of *Scientific American*,
as follows: "How the Milky Way Formed" by Sidney van den Bergh and
James E. Hesser, January 1993; "Our Growing, Breathing Galaxy" by
Bart P. Wakker and Philipp Richter, January 2004; "Refuges for Life in a
Hostile Universe" by Guillermo Gonzalez, Donald Brownlee and Peter D.
Ward, October 2001; "The Paradox of the Sun's Hot Corona" by Bhola N.
Dwivedi and Kenneth J. H. Phillips, June 2001; "The Gas between the
Stars" by Ronald J. Reynolds, January 2002; "The Secrets of Stardust" by
J. Mayo Greenberg, December 2000; "Galaxies behind the Milky Way"
by Renée C. Kraan-Korteweg and Ofer Lahav, October 1998.

First Edition

Library of Congress Cataloging-in-Publication Data

Mysteries of the Milky Way. — 1st ed.
   p. cm. — (Scientific American cutting-edge science)
Includes index.
ISBN-13: 978-1-4042-1404-0 (library binding)
1. Milky Way—Juvenile literature. I. Rosen Publishing Group.
QB857.7.M97 2008
523.1'13—dc22

2007036613

Manufactured in Singapore

Illustration credits: Cover foreground Ron Miller, background © www.
istockphoto.com/Jan Tyler; p. 13 Michael J. Bolte, Lick Observatory;
Johnny Johnson; p. 18 Johnny Johnson; pp. 26, 37 Ron Miller; pp. 49, 68,
89, 109, 116 Don Dixon; p. 51 Sara Chen; source: Nuno C. Santos
Geneva Observatory; p. 56 Sara Chen; p. 104 Cleo Vilett; p. 118 Michael
Goodman; p. 130 Time Moore.

On the cover: The Milky Way.

Table of Contents

Introduction

Viewed from above, it appears as a giant pinwheel of diamond-studded smoke. From Earth, it cuts a pale swath of light across the summer sky. This is the Milky Way, our home galaxy, and it has captivated humankind for millennia. Galileo was the first to formally probe its secrets. Armed with a telescope of his own devising, he determined that the shimmering band was in fact composed of stars. Astronomers have been smitten ever since.

This exclusive book brings together stunning Milky Way discoveries from the past decade. Leading scientists explain how our galaxy formed, how it continues to evolve and why only part of it is habitable. Other articles home in on particular Milky Way elements— our paradoxical sun, cosmic dust and the dynamic interstellar medium. Of course, as fascinating as our galactic neighborhood is, astronomers also yearn to peer beyond it. These efforts, too, are summarized here. We hope that after reading this issue, you'll see our spectacular corner of the cosmos in a different light.

—*The Editors*

I. "How the Milky Way Formed"

By Sidney van den Bergh and James E. Hesser

Its halo and disk suggest that the collapse of a gas cloud, stellar explosions and the capture of galactic fragments may have all played a role.

Attempts to reconstruct how the Milky Way formed and began to evolve resemble an archaeological investigation of an ancient civilization buried below the bustling center of an ever changing modern city. From excavations of foundations, some pottery shards and a few bones, we must infer how our ancestors were born, how they grew old and died and how they may have helped create the living culture above. Like archaeologists, astronomers, too, look at small, disparate clues to determine how our galaxy and others like it were born about a billion years after the big bang and took on their current shapes. The clues consist of the ages of stars and stellar clusters, their distribution and their chemistry—all deduced by looking at such features as color and luminosity. The shapes and physical properties of other galaxies can also provide insight concerning the formation of our own.

The evidence suggests that our galaxy, the Milky Way, came into being as a consequence of the collapse of a vast gas cloud. Yet that cannot be the whole story. Recent observations have forced workers who support the hypothesis of a simple, rapid collapse to modify their idea in important ways. This new information has led other researchers to postulate that several gas cloud fragments merged to create the protogalactic Milky Way, which then collapsed. Other variations on these themes are vigorously maintained. Investigators of virtually all persuasions recognize that the births of stars and supernovae have helped shape the Milky Way. Indeed, the formation and explosion of stars are at this moment further altering the galaxy's structure and influencing its ultimate fate.

Much of the stellar archaeological information that astronomers rely on to decipher the evolution of our galaxy resides in two regions of the Milky Way: the halo and the disk. The halo is a slowly rotating, spherical region that surrounds all the other parts of the galaxy. The stars and star clusters in it are old. The rapidly rotating, equatorial region constitutes the disk, which consists of young stars and stars of intermediate age, as well as interstellar gas and dust. Embedded in the disk are the sweepingly curved arms that are characteristic of spiral galaxies such as the Milky Way. Among the middle-aged stars is our sun, which is located about 25,000 light-years from the galactic center. (When you view the night sky, the galactic center lies in the direction of Sagittarius.) The sun completes an orbit around the center in approximately 200 million years.

That the sun is part of the Milky Way was discovered less than 70 years ago. At the time, Bertil Lindblad of Sweden and the late Jan H. Oort of the Netherlands hypothesized that the Milky Way system is a flattened, differentially rotating galaxy. A few years later John S. Plaskett and Joseph A. Pearce of Dominion Astrophysical Observatory accumulated three decades' worth of data on stellar motions that confirmed the Lindblad-Oort picture.

In addition to a disk and a halo, the Milky Way contains two other subsystems: a central bulge, which consists primarily of old stars, and, within the bulge, a nucleus. Little is known about the nucleus because the dense gas clouds in the central bulge obscure it. The nuclei of some spiral galaxies, including the Milky Way, may contain a large black hole. A black hole in the nucleus of our galaxy, however, would not be as massive as those that seem to act as the powerful cores of quasars.

All four components of the Milky Way appear to be embedded in a large, dark corona of invisible material. In most spiral galaxies the mass of this invisible corona exceeds by an order of magnitude that of all the galaxy's visible gas and stars. Investigators are intensely debating what the constituents of this dark matter might be.

The clues to how the Milky Way developed lie in its components. Perhaps the only widely accepted idea is that the central bulge formed first, through the collapse of a gas cloud. The central bulge, after all, contains mostly massive, old stars. But determining when and how the disk and halo formed is more problematic.

In 1958 Oort proposed a model according to which the population of stars forming in the halo flattened into a thick disk, which then evolved into a thin one. Meanwhile further condensation of stars from the hydrogen left over in the halo replenished that structure. Other astronomers prefer a picture in which these populations are discrete and do not fade into one another. In particular, V. G. Berman and A. A. Suchkov of the Rostov State University in Russia have indicated how the disk and halo could have developed as separate entities.

These workers suggest a hiatus between star formation in the halo and that in the disk. According to their model, a strong wind propelled by supernova explosions interrupted star formation in the disk for a few billion years. In doing so, the wind would have ejected a significant fraction of the mass of the proto-galaxy into intergalactic space. Such a process seems to have prevailed in the Large Magellanic Cloud, one of the Milky Way's small satellite galaxies. There an almost 10-billion-year interlude appears to separate the initial burst of creation of conglomerations of old stars called globular clusters and the more recent epoch of star formation in the disk. Other findings lend additional weight to the notion of distinct galactic components. The nearby spiral M33 contains a halo but no nuclear bulge. This characteristic indicates that a halo is not just an extension of the interior feature, as many thought until recently.

In 1962 a model emerged that served as a paradigm for most investigators. According to its developers—

Olin J. Eggen, now at the National Optical Astronomical Observatories, Donald Lynden-Bell of the University of Cambridge and Allan R. Sandage of the Carnegie Institution—the Milky Way formed when a large, rotating gas cloud collapsed rapidly, in about a few hundred million years. As the cloud fell inward on itself, the protogalaxy began to rotate more quickly; the rotation created the spiral arms we see today. At first, the cloud consisted entirely of hydrogen and helium atoms, which were forged during the hot, dense initial stages of the big bang. Over time the protogalaxy started to form massive, short-lived stars. These stars modified the composition of galactic matter, so that the subsequent generations of stars, including our sun, contain significant amounts of elements heavier than helium.

Although the model gained wide acceptance, observations made during the past three decades have uncovered a number of problems with it. In the first place, investigators found that many of the oldest stars and star clusters in the galactic halo move in retrograde orbits—that is, they revolve around the galactic center in a direction opposite to that of most other stars. Such orbits suggest that the protogalaxy was quite clumpy and turbulent or that it captured sizable gaseous fragments whose matter was moving in different directions. Second, more refined dynamic models show that the protogalaxy would not have collapsed as smoothly as predicted by the simple model; instead the densest parts would have fallen inward much faster than more rarefied regions.

Third, the time scale of galaxy formation may have been longer than that deduced by Eggen and his colleagues. Exploding supernovae, plasma winds pouring from massive, short-lived stars and energy from an active galactic nucleus are all possible factors. The galaxy may also have subsequently rejuvenated itself by absorbing large inflows of pristine intergalactic gas and by capturing small, gas-rich satellite galaxies.

Several investigators have attempted to develop scenarios consistent with the findings. In 1977 Alar Toomre of the Massachusetts Institute of Technology postulated that most galaxies form from the merger of several large pieces rather than from the collapse of a single gas cloud. Once merged in this way, according to Toomre, the gas cloud collapsed and evolved into the Milky Way now seen. Leonard Searle of the Carnegie Institution and Robert J. Zinn of Yale University have suggested a somewhat different picture, in which many small bits and pieces coalesced. In the scenarios proposed by Toomre and by Searle and Zinn, the ancestral fragments may have evolved in chemically unique ways. If stars began to shine and supernovae started to explode in different fragments at different times, then each ancestral fragment would have its own chemical signature. Recent work by one of us (van den Bergh) indicates that such differences do indeed appear among the halo populations.

Discussion of the history of galactic evolution did not advance significantly beyond this point until the 1980s. At that time, workers became able to record more precisely than ever before extremely faint images. This ability is critically important because the physical theories of stellar energy production—and hence the lifetimes and ages of stars—are most secure for so-called main-sequence stars. Such stars burn hydrogen in their cores; in general, the more massive the star, the more quickly it completes its main-sequence life. Unfortunately, this fact means that within the halo the only remaining main-sequence stars are the extremely faint ones. The largest, most luminous ones, which have burned past their main-sequence stage, became invisible long ago. Clusters are generally used to determine age. They are crucial because their distances from the earth can be determined much more accurately than can those of individual stars.

The technology responsible for opening the study of extremely faint halo stars is the charge-coupled device (CCD). This highly sensitive detector produces images electronically by converting light intensity into current. CCDs are far superior in most respects to photographic emulsions, although extremely sophisticated software, such as that developed by Peter B. Stetson of Dominion Astrophysical Observatory, is required to take full advantage of them. So used, the charge-coupled device has yielded a tenfold increase in the precision of measurement of color and luminosity of the faint stars in globular clusters.

Among the most important results of the CCD work done so far are more precise age estimates. Relative age data based on these new techniques have revealed that clusters whose chemistries suggest they were the first to be created after the big bang have the same age to within 500 million years of one another. The ages of other clusters, however, exhibit a greater spread.

The ages measured have helped researchers determine how long it took for the galactic halo to form. For instance, Michael J. Bolte, now at Lick Observatory, carefully measured the colors and luminosities of individual stars in the globular clusters NGC 288 and NGC 362 [see "Color-Luminosity" box]. Comparison between these data and stellar evolutionary calculations shows that NGC 288 is approximately 15 billion years old and that NGC 362 is only about 12 billion years in age. This difference is greater than the uncertain ties in the measurements. The observed age range indicates that the collapse of the outer halo is likely to have taken an order of magnitude longer than the amount of time first envisaged in the simple, rapid collapse model of Eggen, Lynden-Bell and Sandage.

Of course, it is possible that more than one model for the formation of the galaxy is correct. The Eggen–Lynden-Bell–Sandage scenario may apply to the dense bulge and inner halo. The more rarefied outer parts of the galaxy may have developed by the merger of fragments, along the lines theorized by Toomre or by Searle and Zinn. If so, then the clusters in the inner halo would have formed before those in the more tenuous outer regions. The process would account for some of the age differences found for the

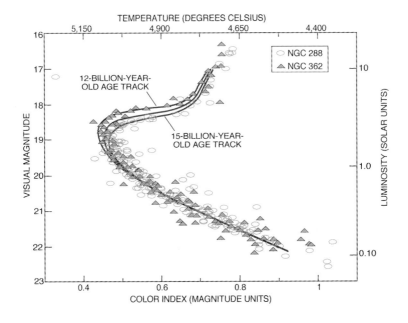

Color-luminosity diagrams can be used to determine stellar ages. The one above compares the plots of stars in globular clusters NGC 288 and NGC 362 with age tracks (*curved lines*) generated by stellar evolution models. The color index, expressed in magnitude units, is a measure of the intensity of blue wavelengths minus visual ones. In general, the brighter the star, the lower the color index; the trend reverses for stars brighter than about visual magnitude 19. The plots suggest the clusters differ in age by about three billion years. The temperature (inversely related to the color index) and luminosity have been set to equal those of NGC 288.

globular clusters. More precise modeling may have to await the improved image quality that modifications to the Hubble Space Telescope cameras will afford.

Knowing the age of the halo is, however, insufficient to ascertain a detailed formation scenario. Investigators need to know the age of the disk as well and then to compare that age with the halo's age. Whereas globular clusters are useful in determining the age of the halo, another type of celestial body—very faint white dwarf stars—can be used to determine the age of the disk. The absence of white dwarfs in the galactic disk near the sun sets a lower limit on the disk's age. White dwarfs, which are no longer producing radiant energy, take a long time to cool, so their absence means that the population in the disk is fairly young—less than about 10 billion years. This value is significantly less than the ages of clusters in the halo and is thus consistent with the notion that the bulk of the galactic disk developed after the halo.

It is, however, not yet clear if there is a real gap between the time when formation of the galactic halo ended and when creation of the old thick disk began. To estimate the duration of such a transitional period between halo and disk, investigators have compared the ages of the oldest stars in the disk with those of the youngest ones in the halo. The oldest known star clusters in the galactic disk, NGC 188 and NGC 6791, have ages of nearly eight billion years, according to Pierre Demarque and David B. Guenther of Yale and Elizabeth M. Green of the University of Arizona. Stetson and his colleagues and Roberto Buonanno of the Astronomical Observatory in Rome and his co-workers examined globular clusters in the halo population. They found the youngest globulars—Palomar 12 and Ruprecht 106—to be about 11 billion years old. If the few billion years' difference between the disk objects and the young globulars is real, then young globulars may be the missing links between the disk and halo populations of the galaxy.

At present, unfortunately, the relative ages of only a few globular clusters have been precisely estimated. As long as this is the case, one can argue that the Milky Way could have tidally captured Palomar 12 and Ruprecht 106 from the Magellanic Clouds. This scenario, proposed by Douglas N. C. Lin of the University of California at Santa Cruz and Harvey B. Richer of the University of British Columbia, would obviate the need for a long collapse time. Furthermore, the apparent age gap between disk and halo might be illusory. Undetected systematic errors may lurk in the age-dating processes. Moreover, gravitational interactions with massive interstellar clouds may have disrupted the oldest disk clusters, leaving behind only younger ones.

Determining the relative ages of the halo and disk reveals much about the sequence of the formation of the galaxy. On the other hand, it leaves open the question of how old the entire galaxy actually is. The answer would provide some absolute framework by which the sequence of formation events can be discerned. Most astronomers who study star clusters favor an age of some 15 to 17 billion years for the oldest clusters (and hence the galaxy).

Confidence that those absolute age values are realistic comes from the measured abundance of radioactive isotopes in meteorites. The ratios of thorium 232 to uranium 235, of uranium 235 to uranium 238 or of uranium 238 to plutonium 244 act as chronometers. According to these isotopes, the galaxy is between 10 and 20 billion years old. Although ages determined by such isotope ratios are believed to be less accurate than those achieved by comparing stellar observations and models, the consistency of the numbers is encouraging.

Looking at the shapes of other galaxies alleviates to some extent the uncertainty of interpreting the galaxy's evolution. Specifically, the study of other galaxies presents a perspective that is unavailable to us as residents of the Milky Way—an external view. We can also compare information from other galaxies to see if the processes that created the Milky Way are unique.

The most immediate observation one can make is that galaxies come in several shapes. In 1925 Edwin P. Hubble found that luminous galaxies could be arranged in a linear sequence according to whether they are elliptical, spiral or irregular. From an evolutionary point of view, elliptical galaxies are the most advanced. They have used up all (or almost all) of their gas to generate stars, which probably range in age from 10 to 15 billion years. Unlike spiral galaxies, ellipticals lack disk structures. The main differences between spiral and irregular galaxies is that irregulars have neither spiral arms nor compact nuclei.

The morphological types of galaxies can be understood in terms of the speed with which gas was used to create stars. Determining the rate of gas depletion would corroborate estimates of the Milky Way's age and history. Star formation in elliptical galaxies appears to have started off rapidly and eciently some 15 billion years ago and then declined sharply. In most irregular galaxies the birth of stars has taken place much more slowly and at a more nearly constant rate. Thus, a significant fraction of their primordial gas still remains.

The rate of star formation in spirals seems to represent a compromise between that in ellipticals and that in irregulars. Star formation in spirals began less rapidly than it did in ellipticals but continues to the present day.

Spirals are further subdivided into categories Sa, Sb and Sc. The subdivisions refer to the relative size of the nuclear bulges and the degree to which the spiral arms coil. Objects of type Sa have the largest nuclear bulges and the most tightly coiled arms. Such spirals also contain some neutral hydrogen gas and a sprinkling of young blue stars. Sb spirals have relatively large populations of young blue stars in their spiral arms. The central bulge, containing old red stars, is less prominent than is the central bulge in spirals of type Sa. Finally, in Sc spirals the light comes mainly from the young blue stars in the spiral arms; the bulge population is inconspicuous or absent. The Milky Way is probably intermediate between types Sb and Sc.

Information from other spirals seems consistent with the data obtained for the Milky Way. Like those in our galaxy, the stars in the central bulges of other spirals arose early. The dense inner regions of gas must have collapsed first. As a result, most of the primordial gas initially present near the centers has turned into stars or has been ejected by supernova-driven winds.

There is an additional kind of evidence on which to build our understanding of how the Milky Way came into existence: the chemical composition of stars. This information helps to pinpoint the relative ages of stellar populations. According to stellar models, the chemistry of a star depends on when it formed. The chemical differences exist because first-generation stars began to "pollute" the protogalaxy with elements heavier than helium. Such so-called heavy elements, or "metals," as astronomers refer to them, were created in the interiors of stars or during supernova explosions. Examining the makeup of stars can provide stellar evolutionary histories that corroborate or challenge age estimates.

Different types of stars and supernovae produce different relative abundances of these metals. Researchers believe that most "iron-peak" elements (those closest to iron in the periodic table) in the galaxy were made in supernovae of type Ia. The progenitors of such super-novae are thought to be pairs of stars, each of which has a mass a few times that of the sun. Other heavy elements—the bulk of oxygen, neon, magnesium, silicon and calcium, among others—originated in supernovae that evolved from single or binaries of massive, short-lived stars. Such stars have initial masses of 10 to 100 solar masses and violently end their lives as supernovae of type Ib, Ic or II.

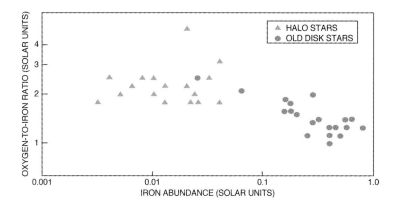

Oxygen-to-iron ratios as a function of metallicity (abundance of iron) for halo and old disk stars indicate different formation histories. The high ratios in metal-deficient halo stars suggest that those stars incorporated the oxygen synthesized in supernovae of types Ib, Ic and II. Type Ia supernovae seem to have contributed material only to the disk stars. Beatriz Barbuy and Marcia Erdelyi-Mendes of the University of São Paulo made the measurements.

Stars that subsequently formed incorporated some of these heavy elements. For instance, approximately 1 to 2 percent of the mass of the sun consists of elements other than hydrogen or helium. Stars in nuclear bulges generally harbor proportionally more heavy elements than do stars in the outer disks and halos. The abundance of heavy elements decreases gradually by a factor of 0.8 for every kiloparsec (3,300 light-years) from the center to the edge of the Milky Way disk. Some 70 percent of the 150 or so known globular clusters in the Milky Way exhibit an average metal content of about one twentieth that of the sun. The remainder shows a mean of about one third that of the sun.

Detailed studies of stellar abundances reveal that the ratio of oxygen to iron-peak elements is larger in halo stars than it is in metal-rich disk stars [see "Oxygen-to-Iron Ratios" box]. This difference suggests the production of heavy elements during the halo phase of galactic evolution was dominated by supernovae of types Ib, Ic and II. It is puzzling that iron-producing type Ia supernovae, some of which are believed to have resulted from progenitor stars with lifetimes as short as a few hundred million years, did not contribute more to the chemical mixture from which halo stars and some globular clusters formed. This failure would seem to imply that the halo collapsed very rapidly— before supernovae of type Ia could contribute their iron to the halo gas.

That idea, however, conflicts with the four-billion-year age spread observed among galactic globular clusters, which implies that the halo collapsed slowly. Perhaps supernova-driven galactic winds swept the iron-rich ejecta from type Ia supernovae into inter-galactic space. Such preferential removal of the ejecta of type Ia supernovae might have occurred if supernovae of types Ib, Ic and II exploded primarily in dense gas clouds. Most of type Ia supernovae then must have detonated in less dense regions, which are more easily swept out by the galactic wind.

Despite the quantity of data, information about metal content has proved insufficient to settle the controversy concerning the time scale of disk and halo formation. Sandage and his colleague Gary A. Fouts of Santa Monica College find evidence for a rather monolithic collapse. On the other hand, John E. Norris and his collaborators at the Australian National Observatory, among others, argue for a significant decoupling between the formation of halo and disk. They also posit a more chaotic creation of the galaxy, similar to that envisaged by Searle and Zinn.

Such differences in interpretation often reflect nearly unavoidable effects arising from the way in which particular samples of stars are selected for study. For example, some stars exhibit chemical compositions similar to those of "genuine" halo stars, yet they have kinematics that would associate them with one of the subcomponents of the disk. As vital as it is, chemical information alone does not resolve ambiguities about the formation of the galactic halo and disk. "Cats and dogs may have the same age and metallicity, but they are still cats and dogs" is the way Bernard Pagel of the Nordic Institute for Theoretical Physics in Copenhagen puts it.

As well as telling us about the past history of our galaxy, the disk and halo also provide insight into the Milky Way's probable future evolution. One can easily calculate that almost all of the existing gas will be consumed in a few billion years. This estimate is based on the rate of star formation in the disks of other spirals and on the assumption that the birth of stars will continue at its present speed. Once the gas has been depleted, no more stars will form, and the disks of spirals will then fade. Eventually the galaxy will consist of nothing more than white dwarfs and black holes encapsulated by the hypothesized dark matter corona.

Several sources of evidence exist for such an evolutionary scenario. In 1978 Harvey R. Butcher of the Kapteyn Laboratory in the Netherlands and Augustus Oemler, Jr., of Yale found that dense clusters of galaxies located about six billion light-years away still contained numerous spiral galaxies. Such spirals are, however, rare or absent in nearby clusters of galaxies. This observation shows that the disks of most spirals in dense clusters must have faded to invisibility during the past six billion years. Even more direct evidence for the swift evolution of galaxies comes from the observation of so-called blue galaxies. These galaxies are rapidly generating large stars. Such blue galaxies seem to be less common now than they were only a few billion years ago.

Of course, the life of spiral galaxies can be extended. Copious infall of hydrogen from intergalactic space might replenish the gas supply. Such infall can occur if a large gas cloud or another galaxy with a substantial gas reservoir is nearby. Indeed, the Magellanic Clouds will eventually plummet into the Milky Way, briefly rejuvenating our galaxy. Yet the Milky Way will not escape its ultimate fate. Like people and civilizations, stars and galaxies leave behind only artifacts in an evolving, ever dynamic universe.

FURTHER READING

Galactic Astronomy: Structure and Kinematics. Dimitri Mihalas and James Binney. W. H. Freeman and Company, 1981.

The Milky Way as a Galaxy. Gerard Gilmore, Ivan R. King and Pieter C. van der Kruit. University Science Books, Mill Valley, Calif., 1990.

The Formation and Evolution of Star Clusters. Edited by Kenneth Janes. Astronomical Society of the Pacific, 1991.

The Stellar Populations of Galaxies. Edited by B. Barbuy and A. Renzini. Kluwer Academic Publishers, Dordrecht, Holland, 1992.

About the Author

SIDNEY VAN DEN BERGH and *JAMES E. HESSER* both work at Dominion Astrophysical Observatory, National Research Council of Canada, in Victoria, British Columbia. Van den Bergh has a longtime interest in the classification and evolution of galaxies and in problems related to the age and size of the universe. He received his undergraduate degree from

Princeton University and a doctorate in astronomy from the University of Göttingen. Hesser's current interests focus on the ages and compositions of globular star clusters, which are among the oldest constituents of the galaxy. He received his B.A. from the University of Kansas and his Ph.D. in atomic and molecular physics from Princeton.

"Our Growing,
2. Breathing Galaxy"

By Bart P. Wakker and Philipp Richter

Long assumed to be a relic of the distant past, the Milky Way turns out to be a dynamic, living object.

Sometimes the hardest things to understand are the things you are most familiar with.

We may know our hometowns intimately, yet visitors or young children may still point out things we have never noticed before. They may not be as attuned to all the minutiae, but they often see the big picture better than longtime residents can. A similar situation faces astronomers who study the Milky Way: we are so deeply embedded in our home galaxy that we cannot see it fully. When we look at other galaxies, we can discern their overall layout but not their detailed workings. When we look at our own, we can readily study the details but perceive the overall structure only indirectly.

Consequently, we have been slow to grasp the big picture of the Milky Way's structure and history. Astronomers were not even sure that the galaxy was a distinct object, only one of many billions, until the 1920s. By the mid-1950s they had painstakingly assembled the picture that most people now have of the Milky Way: a majestic pinwheel of stars and gas. In the 1960s theorists proposed that our galaxy formed

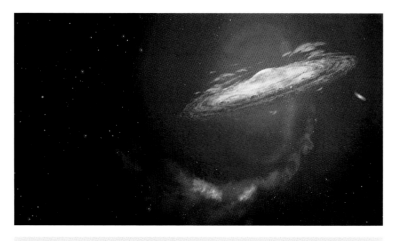

Gulping down gas and cannibalizing its smaller neighbors, the Milky Way galaxy is still in the process of forming.

early in cosmic history—by the most recent estimate, 13 billion years ago—and has remained broadly unchanged ever since.

Gradually, though, it has become clear that the Milky Way is not a finished work but rather a body that is still forming. Like the earlier discoveries, this realization has relied heavily on observing other galaxies and bringing the lessons back home. Most galaxies are now assumed to result from the merging of smaller precursors, and in the case of the Milky Way, we can observe the final stages of this process. Our galaxy is tearing apart small satellite galaxies and incorporating their stars. Meanwhile gas clouds are continually arriving from intergalactic space. No longer can researchers speak of galaxy formation in the past tense.

The evidence for the continuing accretion of gas by the Milky Way involves high-velocity clouds, or HVCs—mysterious clumps of hydrogen, up to 10 million times the mass of the sun and 10,000 light-years across, moving rapidly through the outer regions of the galaxy. HVCs were discovered 41 years ago, but only in the past five years have new data and new ideas provided the evidence that some of them represent infalling gas. HVCs also show that the galaxy is breathing—pushing out gas and then pulling it back in, as if exhaling and inhaling. In addition, the properties of HVCs suggest that a gigantic sphere of hot, tenuous plasma surrounds the galaxy. Astronomers had long suspected the existence of such a sphere, but few thought it would be so large.

Historically, interpreting HVCs has been difficult because being stuck within the galaxy, we have no direct way to know their locations. We can see their

Overview/High-Velocity Clouds

- Since the early 1960s astronomers have thought that the Milky Way and other galaxies were born early in cosmic history and then evolved slowly. Today, however, evidence indicates that galaxies are continuing to grow. They cannibalize their smaller brethren and gulp down fresh gas from intergalactic space.
- In our Milky Way we have a close-up view of the ongoing construction work. The incoming gas takes the form of high-velocity clouds discovered decades ago. Only recently were some of these clouds proved to be fresh material; observationally, they get entangled with circulating gas.
- These clouds come in several guises: clumps of neutral hydrogen reminiscent of intergalactic gas; a stream of gas torn out of nearby small galaxies; and highly ionized hot gas that may be dispersed throughout the intergalactic vicinity.

two-dimensional positions on the sky but lack depth perception. Over the past four decades, this ambiguity has led to many alternative hypotheses, some placing HVCs close to our own stellar neighborhood, others locating them deep in intergalactic space. The recent breakthroughs have occurred mainly because ground-based and orbiting telescopes have finally managed to get a three-dimensional fix on the clouds—and thereby a better perspective on our celestial hometown.

Virgin or Recycled?

Our galaxy contains about 100 billion stars, most of which are concentrated in a thin disk about 100,000 light-years across and 3,000 light-years thick. These stars revolve around the galactic center in nearly circular orbits. The sun, for example, trundles around at nearly 200 kilometers per second. Another 10 billion stars form the galactic "halo," a huge spherical envelope that surrounds the disk. Between the stars lie gas and dust, forming the interstellar medium, most of which also moves in nearly circular orbits around the galactic center and is even more narrowly concentrated in a disk than the stars are. Like a planet's atmosphere, the gas in the medium is densest at its "bottom" (the galactic plane) and thins out with height. But up to about 10 percent of the interstellar medium lies outside the plane and moves up to 400 kilometers per second faster than rotation would imply. This gas constitutes the HVCs.

The story of HVCs began in the mid-1950s, when Guido Münch of the California Institute of Technology discovered dense pockets of gas outside the plane—a clear exception to the rule that the density of gas diminishes with height. Left to themselves, those dense pockets should quickly dissipate, so in 1956 Lyman Spitzer, Jr., of Princeton University proposed that they were stabilized by a hot, gaseous corona that surrounded the Milky Way, a galactic-scale version of the corona around the sun [see "The Coronas of Galaxies," by Klaas S. de Boer and Blair D. Savage; *Scientific American*, August 1982].

Inspired by Spitzer's proposal, Jan Oort of Leiden University in the Netherlands conjectured that the galactic halo might also contain cold gas very far from the galactic plane. A search for radio emission from cold clouds resulted in their discovery in 1963. Unlike the gas found by Münch, these clouds did not follow the overall rotation of the galaxy; instead they seemed to be falling toward the galactic disk at high speed, so they became known as HVCs. A slower-moving but still anomalous type of cloud, an intermediate-velocity cloud, or IVC, was spotted the same year.

Oort later fleshed out his idea and suggested that after the initial formation of the galaxy, gas near the edge of its gravitational sphere of influence was left over. This gas reached the disk only after 10 billion years or more, becoming observable as HVCs. Oort's idea fit in well with models that try to explain the observed chemical composition of the galaxy. Stars produce heavy elements and scatter them into interstellar space when they die. Newly born stars incorporate those elements and produce even more. Therefore, if the galaxy were evolving in isolation, each generation of stars should contain more heavy elements than its predecessors.

Yet most stars in the solar neighborhood, regardless of age, have about the same abundance of heavy elements. The favored explanation for this apparent discrepancy is that the galaxy is not isolated and that interstellar gas is constantly being diluted by more pristine material. Several researchers surmised that some or all of the HVCs represent this fresh gas, but the proposition lacked direct observational evidence.

An alternative hypothesis holds that HVCs have nothing to do with an influx of gas but are instead part of a "galactic fountain." This idea was proposed in the mid-1970s by Paul Shapiro, now at the University of Texas at Austin, and George B. Field of the Harvard-Smithsonian Center for Astrophysics. Gas heated and ionized by massive stars rises out of the disk into the corona, forming an atmosphere. Some regions then cool off, rain back down and become electrically neutral again, setting up a cycle of gas between the disk and the corona. In 1980 Joel Bregman, now at the University of Michigan at Ann Arbor, suggested that HVCs could be the returning gas, and for a while this idea was the leading explanation for their origin.

Going Out with the Tide

Neither Oort's hypothesis nor the fountain model, however, could explain all characteristics of all HVCs. The problem was further complicated by the discovery in the early 1970s of the Magellanic Stream, a filament of gas that arcs around the galaxy. The stream follows the orbits of the Large and Small Magellanic Clouds, two small companion galaxies that revolve around the Milky Way like moons around a planet. Although astronomers usually reserve the term "cloud" for a clump of gas or dust, these full-fledged galaxies containing billions of stars are so named because they resemble clouds in the night sky. They are currently about 150,000 light-years from our galaxy, about as close as they ever get on their highly elongated paths.

The stream behaves in many ways like a string of HVCs. Much of it moves at velocities that are incompatible with normal galactic rotation. Yet it cannot be explained by the two hypotheses described above. According to the most detailed model of the stream, published in 1996 by Lance T. Gardiner of Sun Moon University in South Korea and Masafumi Noguchi of Tohoku University in Japan, the filament is our galaxy's version of the tidal streams that astronomers see around many other galaxies. When the Magellanic Clouds made their previous close approach to the Milky Way, 2.2 billion years ago, the combined force of our galaxy and the Large Magellanic Cloud ripped off some of the gas in the outer parts of the Small Magellanic Cloud. About half the gas was decelerated and lagged behind the Magellanic Clouds in their orbits. The other half was accelerated and pulled ahead of the galaxies, forming what is called a leading arm. A similar process may also be ripping apart some of the Milky Way's other satellite galaxies [see "Conscious of Streams" box].

An alternative model ascribes the stream to frictional forces. If the Milky Way has a very extended corona (much bigger than the one proposed by Spitzer), this corona could strip off gas from the Magellanic Clouds. In either model, however, the Magellanic Clouds have lost large amounts of gas, producing many of the HVCs.

Yet another twist in the saga of HVCs came in 1999, when Leo Blitz of the University of California at Berkeley and his collaborators suggested that they are much farther away than most of their colleagues thought possible. Instead of buzzing through the outskirts of the Milky Way, HVCs could be floating around in the Local Group of galaxies—a conglomeration of the Milky Way, Andromeda and some 40 smaller galaxies that occupies a volume of space roughly four million light-years across. In this case, HVCs would be remnants of the group's, rather than only our galaxy's, formation.

Similar ideas had been put forward more than 30 years ago and excluded because gas clouds should not be stable at the proposed distances. Blitz conjectured that HVCs are not, in fact, clouds of gas but clumps of dark matter with a small amount of gas mixed in. If so, HVCs are 10 times as massive as astronomers

Concious of Streams

Most of the Milky Way is as thoroughly mixed as a well-stirred gravy. Two stars that originated in the same region may be located in completely different parts of the sky today. But during the past few years, astronomers have found groups of stars that move in unison, forming what they call stellar streams. They are like lumps that a cook has just thrown into a pot but that have not had time to mix in.

The streams are believed to be the remnants of satellite galaxies of the Milky Way that were torn apart by tides, the same process that formed some of the high-velocity clouds. The streams thus trace a flow of stars from dwarf galaxies to the Milky Way. They differ from the Magellanic Stream, which consists of gas rather than stars. They represent independent evidence for the ongoing growth of our galaxy.

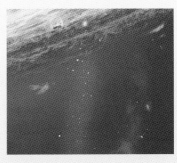

One spectacular example is a stream of stars being pulled off the Sagittarius dwarf spheroidal galaxy, which was discovered in 1994 by Rodrigo Ibata of the Strasbourg Observatory in France and his colleagues [see *artist's conception to the right*]. More recently, several other stellar streams were found in the data gathered by the Sloan Digital Sky Survey, a program to map a large portion of the sky systematically. One may be related to the Canis Major dwarf galaxy, which Ibata, Nicolas Martin of Strasbourg and their collaborators discovered [in 2003]. Over the past two billion years, this galaxy has been stretched into a spiraling ring of stars along the galactic plane. —*B.W. and P.R.*

---

had assumed and therefore able to hold themselves together. An attractive feature of this hypothesis is that it alleviates what has become a major embarrassment for astronomers—namely, that models of galaxy formation predict more leftover dark matter halos than have been found [see "The Life Cycle of Galaxies," by Guinevere Kauffmann and Frank van den Bosch; *Scientific American*, June 2002]. HVCs could be the missing leftovers.

Getting Warmer

Thus, astronomers entered the third millennium with four hypotheses for HVCs: fresh gas left over from galaxy formation, gas cycling through a galactic fountain, shreds of the Magellanic Clouds, or intergalactic amalgams of gas and dark matter. Each hypothesis had bits and pieces of supporting evidence, but researchers needed new data to break the deadlock, and since the mid-1990s they have made major progress.

First, they have completed an all-sky survey for radio emission from neutral hydrogen, which traces gas at temperatures of about 100 kelvins. Aad Hulsbosch of the University of Nijmegen and one of us (Wakker), using the Dwingeloo radio telescope in the Netherlands, finished the northern half of this survey in 1988. Ricardo Morras and his collaborators, using the Villa Elisa radio telescope in Argentina, covered the southern sky in 2000. A third survey, by Dap Hartmann and Butler Burton of Leiden Observatory, became available in 1997 and mapped all of the Milky Way's neutral hydrogen, including both HVCs and IVCs.

A further contribution came from observations in visible light, made by instruments such as the Wisconsin Hydrogen-Alpha Mapper [see "The Gas between the Stars," by Ronald J. Reynolds; *Scientific American*, January 2002]. Although neutral hydrogen does not shine at visible wavelengths, ionized gas does, and the outer parts of HVCs are ionized by far-ultraviolet light from the Milky Way and other objects. The radiation also heats the clouds' exteriors to 8,000 kelvins. The amount of visible light is a measure of the intensity of the radiation field surrounding the HVC, which in turn depends on its distance from the galactic disk. Thus, these observations offer a rough way to estimate the location of HVCs.

The most important progress has come from observations of spectral absorption lines in HVCs. Instead of looking for light given off by the gas, this work analyzes light blocked by the gas—specific atoms filter out specific wavelengths of light. Three observatories have made the largest contributions: the La Palma Observatory in the Canary Islands, the Hubble Space Telescope and the Far Ultraviolet Spectroscopic Explorer (FUSE), launched in 1999.

Using such data, Laura Danly, now at the University of Denver, and her collaborators put limits on the distance to an IVC 11 years ago. More recently, Hugo van Woerden of the University of Groningen in the Netherlands and his collaborators gauged the distance to an HVC for the first time [see "Peeking Behind the Clouds" box]. Meanwhile we and our colleagues measured the chemical composition of the clouds, rounding out the information needed to distinguish among the various hypotheses.

A very warm component of HVCs emerged in data from FUSE. This satellite detected absorption by highly ionized oxygen (specifically, oxygen atoms that have lost five of their eight electrons), which implies a temperature of about 300,000 kelvins. Such temperatures can occur where cool (100 kelvins) neutral hydrogen comes into contact with extremely hot (one million kelvins) gas. Alternatively, the presence of gas at 300,000 kelvins shows that the extremely hot gas is cooling down. Together with Blair D. Savage of the University of Wisconsin–Madison and Kenneth Sembach of the Space Telescope Science Institute in Baltimore, we have traced this component of HVCs.

Complex Behavior

Having explored all these new data, we can now present a coherent picture of HVCs. We begin with two of the largest, known as complexes A and C, which were the first HVCs discovered back in 1963. Complex A is 25,000 to 30,000 light-years away, which clearly puts it in the galactic halo. The distance to complex C remains uncertain: at least 14,000 light-years but probably no more than 45,000 light-years above the galactic plane.

The two clouds are deficient in heavy elements, having about a tenth of the concentration found in the sun. The nitrogen content of complex C is especially low, about 1/50 of the sun's. The paucity of nitrogen suggests that the heavy elements came mostly from high-mass stars, which produce less nitrogen relative to other heavy elements than low-mass stars do. In fact, recent models of the young universe predict that the earliest stars are uncommonly heavy. Complex C thus appears to be a fossil from the ancient universe.

Brad Gibson of Swinburne University in Melbourne, Australia, has looked at a different part of complex C and measured a heavy-element concentration that was twice as high as our earlier results. This variation in composition indicates that complex C has begun to mix with other gas clouds in the galactic halo, which have higher concentrations of heavy elements. In addition, Andrew Fox and his collaborators at Wisconsin used the data for highly ionized oxygen and other ions to show that the gas at 300,000 kelvins in complex C represents an interface between hot and cool gas. We seem to be catching complex C in the process of assimilating into the galaxy.

Clouds such as complexes A and C thus provide the first direct evidence for the infall of fresh gas. Complex C brings between 0.1 and 0.2 solar mass of new material every year, and complex A represents about half of that. This is 10 to 20 percent of the total needed to dilute galactic gas and account for the chemical composition of stars. Other HVCs may make up the remainder. It is somewhat unclear, though, whether the ultimate source of this gas is a remnant halo (as proposed by Oort), deep intergalactic space, or even a small dwarf galaxy that the Milky Way swallowed.

A Multiplicity of Origins

The results eliminate three of the hypotheses for the origin of complexes A and C. The fountain hypothesis implies that they originate in the disk and have a composition similar to that of the sun, which is not the case. The Magellanic Stream hypothesis also gets the heavy-element content wrong. Finally, the dark matter hypothesis fails because these two HVCs do not lie in intergalactic space. It turns out, however, that these three explanations are not completely incorrect. We simply have to look elsewhere to find where they apply.

For a long time, IVCs stood in the shadow of the more flashy and mysterious HVCs. Several teams have now measured their composition, and it matches that of gas in the disk. Moreover, IVCs lie some 4,000 light-years above the plane, the place where fountains would operate. Both facts indicate that they, rather than HVCs, represent the return flow of a fountain.

A piece of corroborating evidence has been the detection of hydrogen molecules in IVCs. Forming these molecules in space requires interstellar dust grains, which will be sufficiently abundant only if the ambient gas is chemically enriched. In line with this idea, molecular hydrogen was not found in complex C. Thus, IVCs are recycled gas from within the galaxy, whereas HVCs are primarily gas from outside.

As for the Magellanic Stream hypothesis, at least one HVC does seem to be a castoff from the stream. Its composition is similar to that of the Small Magellanic Cloud, as Limin Lu and his co-workers at Wisconsin found in 1998. The HVC is located in the leading arm of the stream, meaning that whatever pulled it off the Small

Magellanic Cloud also accelerated it. Frictional forces cannot do that; only tidal forces can. Lu's discovery finally settles the question of the origin of the stream.

Frictional forces may still be important, however. FUSE found highly ionized oxygen associated with the Magellanic Stream, suggesting that it, too, is embedded

Peeking Behind the Clouds

High-velocity clouds stymied astronomers for decades because their distances and compositions were uncertain. The only known technique to measure these properties is the absorption-line method. Stars and galaxies located behind HVCs act as bulbs that shine through the clouds from behind. Most of the light passes through the clouds, but a few wavelengths are absorbed, allowing properties of the clouds to be measured.

If the spectrum of a star contains absorption lines, it means a cloud must be sitting between us and the star. The distance to the star sets an upper limit on the distance to the cloud. Conversely, the lack of an absorption line implies a lower limit on the distance to the cloud. These limits assume that other factors can be ruled out: uncertainties in the stellar distance, lack of enough heavy elements to produce a detectable absorption line, and absorption lines created by material within the star itself.

To determine HVC distances, the most useful lightbulbs are so-called RR Lyrae variables and blue horizontal branch (BHB) stars. They are numerous, their distances can be measured accurately, and few of their spectral lines overlap with those of the clouds. In principle, the absorption lines of any element could be used. To determine the heavy element content, however, the best measurements rely on the spectral lines of neutral oxygen and ionized sulfur. These lines lie in the ultraviolet part of the spectrum, requiring properly equipped satellites such as the Hubble Space Telescope or Far Ultraviolet Spectroscopic Explorer (FUSE). In this case, the best lightbulbs are distant active galaxies such as quasars, because they often have featureless spectra and are brighter ultraviolet emitters than stars.

A single star or galaxy can illuminate more than one gas cloud. Each cloud moves at a different velocity, so each absorbs at a slightly different wavelength because of the Doppler effect. To distinguish the clouds requires a spectrometer with high spectral resolution, which in turn requires a large telescope.   —B.W. and P.R.

in hot gas. The galactic corona must therefore extend much farther out than was originally proposed by Spitzer—out to a few hundred thousand light-years, rather than a few thousand. This corona is not dense enough to strip gas from the Magellanic Clouds, but once the gas has been drawn out by tidal forces, friction with the corona causes it to decelerate, slowly rain down on the galaxy and contribute to the growth of the Milky Way.

Similarly, the dark matter hypothesis, although it does not explain complexes A and C, may fit into the broader scheme of things. Blitz originally proposed that the intergalactic HVCs weigh 10 million to 100 million solar masses. Yet such clouds have not been detected in nearby galaxy groups similar to the Local Group, even though observations are now sensitive enough to do so. Furthermore, the hypothesis predicts that visible-light emission from HVCs should be too faint to detect, but in almost all cases that this emission has been looked for, it has been detected. Finally, theoretical arguments show that if the HVCs are distant, they must be either fully ionized or extremely massive, and both options are inconsistent with observations. It thus appears that HVCs are not the predicted population of dark matter clouds.

Robert Braun of Dwingeloo Observatory and Butler Burton and Vincent de Heij of Leiden instead propose that the Milky Way and Andromeda galaxies are surrounded by several hundred small clouds made mostly of dark matter and ionized gas, with a small fraction of neutral hydrogen. These clouds would weigh at most 10 million solar masses, and rather than roaming throughout the Local Group, most would stay within half a million light-years of the main galaxies.

Although neutral HVCs do not appear to be dispersed throughout the Local Group, other types of high-velocity gas may be. The highly ionized gas in one HVC lies far outside the Milky Way. FUSE has also discovered high-velocity, highly ionized oxygen on its own, without any neutral gas. Similar clouds of hot gas have been found elsewhere in the universe by Todd M. Tripp of Princeton and his co-workers. This hot gas may constitute a filament running through intergalactic space. Such filaments show up in simulations of the broad-scale evolution of the cosmos [see "The Emptiest Places," by Evan Scannapieco, Patrick Petitjean and Tom Broadhurst; *Scientific American*, October 2002], and the total amount of matter in these filaments may be larger than that in all galaxies combined, forming a reservoir that the Milky Way can draw on to make new stars.

The HVCs surrounding the Milky Way remind us that we are living in a galaxy that is still forming and evolving. Originally our galaxy was surrounded by many smaller satellite galaxies and a lot of leftover gas. Over the past several billion years, it has incorporated most of those satellites. It may also have accreted much of the pristine gas from its intergalactic environs, and plenty of gas may still lie out there. Gas is still trickling in, taking the form of HVCs. At the same time, the galaxy expels gas loaded with heavy elements into its halo and maybe even into intergalactic space.

Within the next 10 or so billion years, more satellite galaxies will merge with the Milky Way, forming more of the stellar streams now being discovered in the halo. Our galaxy is on a collision course with the Andromeda galaxy. We cannot tell exactly how the Milky Way, or what is left of it, will look in the distant future, but we know that its formation has not come to an end yet.

More to Explore

High-Velocity Clouds. Bart P. Wakker and Hugo van Woerden in *Annual Review of Astronomy and Astrophysics*, Vol. 35, pages 217–266; September 1997.

A Confirmed Location in the Galactic Halo for the High-Velocity Cloud "Chain A." Hugo van Woerden, Ulrich J. Schwarz, Reynier F. Peletier, Bart P. Wakker and Peter M. W. Kalberla in *Nature*, Vol. 400, pages 138–141; July 8, 1999. Available online at **arXiv.org/abs/astro-ph/9907107**.

Accretion of Low-Metallicity Gas by the Milky Way. Bart P. Wakker, J. Chris Howk, Blair D. Savage, Hugo van Woerden, Steve L. Tufte, Ulrich J. Schwarz, Robert Benjamin, Ronald J. Reynolds, Reynier F. Peletier and Peter M. W. Kalberla in

Nature, Vol. 402, No. 6760; pages 388–390; November 25, 1999.

The Formation and Evolution of the Milky Way. Cristina Chiappini in *American Scientist*, Vol. 89, No. 6, pages 506–515; November–December 2001.

A Far Ultraviolet Spectroscopic Explorer Survey of Molecular Hydrogen in Intermediate-Velocity Clouds in the Milky Way Halo. P. Richter, B. P. Wakker, B. D. Savage and K. R. Sembach in *Astrophysical Journal*, Vol. 586, No. 1, pages 230–248; March 20, 2003. **arXiv.org/abs/astro-ph/0211356.**

Highly Ionized High-Velocity Gas in the Vicinity of the Galaxy. K. R. Sembach, B. P. Wakker, B. D. Savage, P. Richter, M. Meade, J. M. Shull, E. B. Jenkins, G. Sonneborn and H. W. Moos in *Astrophysical Journal*, Supplement Series, Vol. 146, No. 1, pages 165–208; May 2003. **arXiv.org/abs/astro-ph/0207562.**

About the Authors

BART P. WAKKER and *PHILIPP RICHTER* are observers, primarily in the ultraviolet and radio bands of the electromagnetic spectrum. They joined forces to investigate high-velocity clouds in late 1999, when Richter took up a postdoctoral position at the University of Wisconsin–Madison, where Wakker was doing research. Wakker traces his interest in astronomy to the *Apollo 8* moonflight. He did his doctoral thesis on HVCs at the University of Groningen in the Netherlands, then spent five years at the University of Illinois before moving to Wisconsin in 1995. Richter received his Ph.D. from the University of Bonn in Germany, where he studied diffuse molecular gas in the Magellanic Clouds and the halo of the Milky Way. After leaving Wisconsin in 2002, he worked at the Arcetri Astrophysical Observatory in Florence, Italy, and recently returned to Bonn.

"Refuges for Life in
3. a Hostile Universe"

By Guillermo Gonzalez, Donald Brownlee and
   Peter D. Ward

Only part of our galaxy is fit for advanced life.

In science-fiction stories, interstellar travelers visit exotic locales in the Milky Way and meet with interesting aliens. You name the place, and someone has put a civilization there: the galactic center, a globular cluster, a star-forming region, a binary star system, a red dwarf star. Part of the reason that sci-fi writers have to be so inventive is that scientists keep spoiling the fun. It used to be quite respectable to speculate about intelligent beings on the moon, Mars, Venus, Jupiter or even the sun, but nowadays canal-building Martians and cool oases inside the sun are merely quaint notions. As writers go ever farther afield to situate their characters, scientists are not far behind. Researchers are now casting a skeptical eye on musings about the prevalence of intelligent life throughout the Milky Way. Just as most of the solar system is hostile to multicellular organisms, the same may be true of much of the galaxy.

Within a given planetary system, astronomers describe the optimal locations for life in terms of the circumstellar habitable zone (CHZ). Although its definition has varied, the CHZ is generally considered to be the region around a star where liquid water can persist on the surface of a terrestrial, or Earth-like, planet for at least a few billion years. The zone is ring-shaped [see "Habitable Zone" box]. Its inner boundary is the closest that a planet can orbit its host star without losing its oceans to space. In the most extreme case, a runaway greenhouse effect might take hold and boil off the oceans (as happened on Venus). The outer boundary is the farthest a planet can roam before its oceans freeze over. From basic stellar theory, astronomers can estimate the size of the CHZ for a star of any mass [see "How Climate Evolved on the Terrestrial Planets," by James F. Kasting, Owen B. Toon and James B. Pollack; *Scientific American*, February 1988].

Overview/Habitable Zone

- What does a planet need to support complex life-forms? Astronomers have generally focused on the stability of surface water—which is possible only within a certain range of distances from the planet's star, a region known as the circumstellar habitable zone. But in discovering extrasolar planets over the past five years or so, researchers have come to appreciate a broader set of conditions.
- Ideally, the star and its planetary retinue should orbit within a certain range of distances from the center of the galaxy. Too far, and the nebula from which the star emerged will lack the heavy elements out of which planets are made. Too close, and hazards such as orbital instabilities, cometary collisions and exploding stars will nip ecosystems in the bud. The sun's position is just right.
- All this suggests that complex life is rare in the galaxy.

Obviously, many other factors also contribute to the habitability of a planet, including the ellipticity of its orbit, the company of a large moon and the presence of giant planets, let alone the details of its biology. But if a planet orbits outside the zone, none of these minutiae is likely to matter. Similarly, it doesn't make much difference where the CHZ is located if the planetary system as a whole resides in a hostile part of the galaxy.

Thus, in 1999 we proposed the concept of a galactic equivalent to the CHZ: the galactic habitable zone (GHZ). The GHZ defines the most hospitable places in the Milky Way—those that are neither too close nor too far from the galactic center. We are not the first to consider habitability in this broader context. For the past decade Virginia Trimble of the University of Maryland and the University of California at Irvine has been writing about the connection between galactic chemical composition and the conditions required for life. But in recent years, there has been a huge break-through: the discovery of giant, Jupiter-size planets around sunlike stars. Not every sunlike star has such a planet. In fact, the giant planets discovered to date are primarily found around stars that are rich in chemical elements heavier than helium—what astronomers call "metals." This correlation suggests that metal content is an important factor in forming giant planets. (At present, the leading search technique cannot detect Earth-size planets.) At the same time, astronomers have gained a new and sobering appreciation of how deadly our galaxy can be, filled as it is with exploding stars and stellar close encounters. Even where planets do exist, they may not be fit for complex life-forms.

Where's the Wherewithal?

The boundaries of the galactic habitable zone are set by two requirements: the availability of material to build a habitable planet and adequate seclusion from cosmic threats. The story of how chemical elements came to be assembled into Earth is one told by modern cosmology, stellar astrophysics and planetary science. The big bang produced hydrogen and helium and little else. Over the next 10 billion years or so, stars cooked this raw mix into a rich stew of elements. Within the interstellar medium, the ratio of the number of metal atoms to the number of hydrogen atoms—that is, the "metallicity"—gradually increased to its present value.

These metals are the building blocks of Earth-like planets, and their abundance affects the size of the planets that can form. Size, in turn, determines whether a planet can retain an atmosphere and sustain geologic activity. Moreover, without enough metals, no giant planets can form at all, because they coalesce around a rocky core of a certain minimum size. Observations of extrasolar planets are beginning to define the required metallicity for building giant planets. No such planet has been found around any star with a metallicity of less than 40 percent of the sun's. In a study reported last year, the Hubble Space Telescope failed to detect

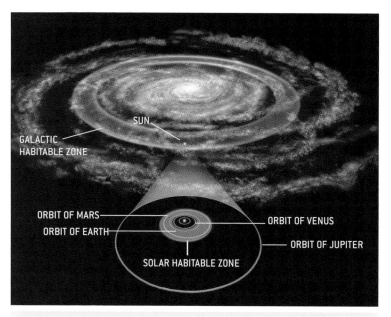

Habitable zone of the Milky Way excludes the dangerous inner regions and the metal-poor outer regions of our galaxy. It is analogous to the habitable zone on the much smaller scale of our solar system (*inset*). Neither zone has sharp boundaries.

any planets in the globular cluster 47 Tucanae, whose stars have metallicities of 25 percent of the solar value [see "Searching for Shadows of Other Earths," by Laurance R. Doyle, Hans-Jörg Deeg and Timothy M. Brown; *Scientific American*, September 2000].

Conversely, too high a metallicity can also be a problem. Terrestrial planets will be larger and, because of their stronger gravity, richer in volatile compounds and poorer in topographic relief. That combination will make them more likely to be completely covered with water, to the detriment of life. On Earth, the mix of land and sea is important for atmospheric temperature control and other processes. High metallicity also increases the density of the protoplanetary disk and thereby induces the giant planets to shift position [see "Migrating Planets," by Renu Malhotra; *Scientific American*, September 1999]. A by-product of this orbital migration is that it will fling any smaller, Earth-like bodies out of the system altogether or shove them into the sun. As the elephants move around, the ants get crushed.

In a recent study, Charles H. Lineweaver of the University of New South Wales in Australia explored the dependence of planet formation and migration on metallicity. He assumed that the probability of forming a terrestrial planet is proportional to the metallicity of the parent star, because both the star and the planet arose from the same cloud of dust and gas. From the extra-solar planet statistics, he inferred that the probability of giant-planet migration rises steeply with increasing metallicity, with migration inevitable if the metallicity is 300 percent of the solar value. Although Lineweaver's calculations are tentative, they suggest that a metallicity near the sun's may be optimal for the production of Earth-mass planets in stable orbits.

Through Thick and Thin

Only part of the Milky Way satisfies this requirement. Astronomers usually subdivide the Milky Way into four overlapping regions: halo, bulge, thick disk and thin disk. Stars in each region orbit the galactic center much as planets in our solar system orbit the sun. The halo and thick disk tend to contain older, metal-poor stars; it is unlikely that terrestrial planets as large as Earth have formed around them. Stars in the bulge have

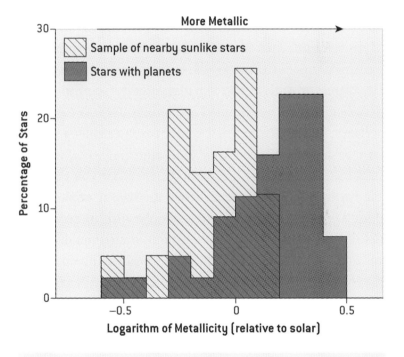

Surveys of extrasolar planets conducted by astronomers have revealed how important the supply of planet-building material is. As this histogram shows, the stars that are parents to giant planets (*solid area*) tend to have a greater abundance of heavy elements ("metals") than the average nearby sunlike star does (*lined*).

a wide range of metallicities, but cosmic radiation levels are higher there.

The thin disk is the sun's home. The metallicity of its gas declines with distance from the galactic center. At the sun's location, about 8.5 kiloparsecs (28,000 light-years) out, it is decreasing at 17 percent per kiloparsec. The logarithm of the metallicity (which astronomers give in units called "dex," the sun having a value of 0 dex, by definition) falls off linearly with distance, with a slope of –0.07 dex per kiloparsec. Observers measure the metallicity gradient using spectral features in various classes of stars and nebulae. The different indicators have converged onto the same answer only within the past three or four years, and galaxies similar to the Milky Way are now known to have similar disk metallicity gradients.

The gradient is an outcome of variations in the star-formation rate. Farther from the center of the galaxy there is proportionately less gas and therefore less star formation. Consequently, the outer reaches of the galaxy have built up less metal than the inner parts. In the galaxy as a whole, the star-formation rate peaked about eight billion to 10 billion years ago and has been declining ever since. Today the metallicity in the solar neighborhood is increasing by about 8 percent every billion years. As the gas supply dwindles, the metallicity will grow at an ever slower rate.

Taking into account the disk metallicity gradient and its evolution, we can place rough limits on the

GHZ both in space and in time [see "Location of Habitable Zone" box]. Stars forming today with a metallicity of between 60 and 200 percent of the sun's value generally reside between 4.5 and 11.5 kiloparsecs from the galactic center—a region that contains only about 20 percent of the stars in the galaxy. Moreover, the typical star in the solar neighborhood did not reach the 60 percent threshold until five billion to six billion years ago. The sun itself is about 40 percent richer in metal than other stars formed at the same time and location in the disk. This increased metal content may have given life on Earth a head start.

Iron Curtains

One potential counterargument is that the correlation of metallicity and detected planets is not the same as causation. Perhaps the causation goes in the opposite direction: instead of high stellar metallicity explaining the presence of giant planets, the presence of giant planets might explain the high stellar metallicity. This would happen if they tended to fall into the stars, enriching their metal content. Most astronomers now think that stars do gobble up planets and smaller bodies. But the outer convective layers of sunlike stars are so massive and so well mixed that they would need to devour an unreasonable amount of planetary material to fully account for the high metallicities seen among stars with planets.

Another rejoinder is that the correlation might be an observational bias. It is harder to spot planets around metal-poor stars; the leading planet search method relies on stellar spectral lines, which are weaker when a star has less metal. But the detection efficiency does not suffer appreciably until a star's metallicity drops below about 10 percent of the sun's value—which is well below the 40 percent threshold needed for giant planets. The observed correlation with planets is quite real.

Metallicity is not the only compositional prerequisite for habitable planets; the relative abundances of different elements matter, too. The most abundant elements on Earth were produced primarily in supernova explosions, of which there are two basic types. Type I events, most of which result from the detonation of a white dwarf star, produce mainly iron, nickel and cobalt. Type II supernovae, which entail the implosion of a massive star, mostly synthesize oxygen, silicon, magnesium, calcium and titanium. Crucially, type II events are also the sole natural source of the very heaviest elements, such as thorium and uranium.

Because star formation in our galaxy is tapering off, the overall rate of supernova explosions is declining—as is the ratio of type II to type I events. Type II supernovae involve short-lived massive stars, so their rate closely tracks the star-formation rate. The rate of type I supernovae, on the other hand, depends on the production of longer-lived intermediate-mass stars, so it responds more slowly to changes in the star-formation rate.

As a result of the shifting supernova ratio, new sunlike stars are richer in iron than those that formed five billion years ago. All else being equal, this implies that a terrestrial planet forming today will have a proportionately larger iron core than Earth does. It will also have, in 4.5 billion years, about 40 percent less heat from the decay of potassium, thorium and uranium. The heat generated by these radioactive isotopes is what drives plate tectonics, which plays an essential role in the geochemical cycle that regulates the amount of carbon dioxide in our atmosphere. Perhaps terrestrial planets forming today would be single-plate planets like Venus and Mars. The lack of plate tectonics on Venus contributes to its hellish conditions [see "Global Climate Change on Venus," by Mark A. Bullock and David H. Grinspoon; *Scientific American*, March 1999]. But we do not yet understand all the ways a planet's geology depends on its internal heat flow.

Danger, Danger

Even if you manage to get all the necessary atoms in the right place at the right time to build an Earth, you may not be justified in sticking a "habitable" label on it. A planet must also be kept reasonably safe from threats. These threats can be put into one of two categories: impacts by asteroids and comets, and blasts of radiation.

In our solar system the frequency of asteroid impacts depends on the details of Jupiter's orbit and formation;

the rest of the galaxy has no direct effect. The cometary threat, on the other hand, is quite sensitive to the galactic environment. Comets are thought to reside in two long-term reservoirs, the Kuiper belt (which starts just beyond Neptune) and the Oort cloud (which extends halfway to the nearest star). Other stars probably have similar retinues. Infrared observations of young nearby stars indicate that most are surrounded by excess dust, consistent with the presence of Kuiper-belt objects. More recently, detection of water vapor around the highly evolved luminous star IRC+10216 has been interpreted as evidence of evaporating comets. Changes in the shapes of certain spectral lines in Beta Pictoris, a young star with a dust disk, could be caused by infalling comets.

Because Oort-cloud comets are only weakly bound to the sun, it doesn't take much to deflect them toward the inner planets. A tug from galactic tides, giant molecular clouds or passing stars can do the trick [see "The Oort Cloud," by Paul R. Weissman; *Scientific American*, September 1998]. The frequency of such perturbations depends on our position in the Milky Way. As one goes toward the galactic center, the density of stars increases, so there are more close encounters. Moreover, a planetary system forming out of a metal-rich cloud will probably contain more comets than one forming out of a cloud with less metal. Thus, planetary systems in the inner galaxy should suffer higher comet influxes than the solar system does. Although the outer Oort cloud in such a system will become depleted more

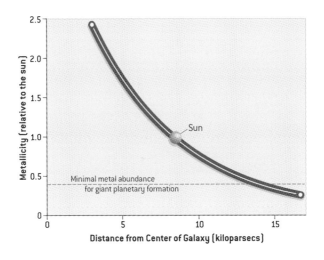

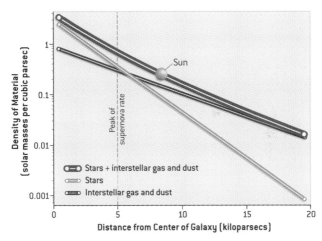

Location of habitable zone is determined by a balance between the supply of plant-building material and the prevalence of threats. The supply falls off with distance from the galactic center (*top*), while the density of stars—a proxy for perils such as stellar explosions and close encounters—also decreases with distance (*bottom*). An acceptable compromise is reached somewhere in the middle, although astronomers cannot yet pin down the precise location.

rapidly, it will also be replenished more rapidly from the inner cometary reservoirs.

High-energy radiation, too, is a bigger problem in the inner regions of the galaxy. Up to a point, a planet's magnetic field can fend off most particle radiation and its ozone layer can screen out dangerous electromagnetic radiation. But sufficiently energetic radiation can ionize the atmosphere and generate nitrogen oxides in amounts capable of wiping out the ozone layer. Energetic radiation hitting the atmosphere can also let loose a deadly rain of secondary particles.

The nastiest radiation events are, in order of decreasing duration, active galactic nucleus outbursts, supernovae and gamma-ray bursts. The nucleus of the Milky Way is currently relatively inactive; the supermassive black hole at the heart of our galaxy appears to be dormant. But observations of other galaxies suggest that central black holes occasionally turn on when a star or cluster wanders too close and is pulled to its death. The result is a burst of high-energy electromagnetic and particle radiation. Most of the radiation is emitted in a jet along the rotation axis of the galaxy, but many of the charged particles will spiral along the galaxy's magnetic field lines and fill its volume. The worst place to be during such an outburst is in the bulge. Not only would the overall radiation levels be high, the stars there would tend to have highly inclined and elliptical orbits that could bring them close to the nucleus or jet.

Supernovae and gamma-ray bursts are also more threatening in the inner galaxy, simply because of the higher concentration of stars there. Observations of supernova remnants indicate that supernovae peak at about 60 percent of the sun's distance from the galactic center, where they are about 1.6 times more frequent than at our location. The threat from gamma-ray bursts remains uncertain; astronomers do not know what triggers these gargantuan explosions or how tightly they beam their radiation. We could just be lucky to have avoided such a death ray so far.

Radiation can also steal life from the crib. Sunlike stars are not born in isolation but rather are often surrounded by both low- and high-mass stars. The high levels of ultraviolet radiation emitted by the latter erode circumstellar disks around nearby stars, reducing their chances of forming giant planets. John Bally of the University of Colorado at Boulder and his colleagues have estimated that only about 10 percent of stars avoid this kind of harassment. This could explain why a mere 3 percent of nearby sunlike stars are found to have giant planets.

All these threats imply a fairly broad habitable zone with fuzzy boundaries. But if we include proximity to the corotation circle as another requirement, then the GHZ could be very narrow. The corotation circle is where the orbital period of a star equals the rotation period of the galaxy's spiral arm pattern. When a star orbits at or very near the corotation circle, spiral arm crossings are less frequent. It will take longer to cross a spiral arm, but what is important is the relatively long period between crossings. Recent measurements of the dynamics of stars near the sun indicate that the sun orbits very near the corotation circle. The spiral arms may look pretty, but they are best appreciated from afar, because the intense star formation and giant molecular clouds within the arms multiply the risks to complex life-forms.

Paradox Lost

At this stage of our research, we are still some way from filling in the details of the GHZ. Continuing studies of comets, galactic nuclei, supernovae, gamma-ray bursts and stellar dynamics will help pinpoint the threats to life. Even now, however, we have a broad picture of the GHZ. The inner regions of the galaxy suffer from orbital instabilities, radiation bursts and cometary perturbations. The outer regions are safer, but because of the lower metallicity, terrestrial planets are typically smaller there. The GHZ appears to be an annulus in the disk at roughly the sun's location [see "Habitable Zone" box]. The GHZ is a probabilistic concept: not every planet inside the zone is habitable (and not every planet outside is sterile). But the probability is much greater inside. The GHZ has been slowly creeping out- ward, as interstellar gas reaches solar metallicity.

The GHZ concept has important implications for searches for extraterrestrial intelligence. It can, for example, identify the most probable places for complex life to form, so that researchers can direct their searches accordingly. We can already say with some confidence that globular clusters, the outer disk and the galactic center make poor targets.

The GHZ concept also has implications for the debate swirling around the Fermi Paradox: If our galaxy is teeming with other civilizations, we should see some evidence of their existence; we do not, so perhaps we are alone [see "Where Are They?" by Ian Crawford; *Scientific American*, July 2000]. One of the arguments proposed to avoid that conclusion is that ETs may have no motivation to leave their home world and scatter signs of their presence through space. But if our ideas about the GHZ are correct, we live within an especially comfortable region of the Milky Way. Any civilization seeking a new world would, no doubt, place our solar system on their home-shopping list. The GHZ theory also weakens the argument that the galaxy is so big that interstellar explorers or colonizers have passed us by. The GHZ may be large, but it is just a part of the entire galaxy, and any galactic travelers would tend to roam around the annulus rather than haphazardly through the galaxy.

Furthermore, the GHZ concept constrains habitability not just in space but also in time. The Milky Way used to be pummeled by supernovae and an active nucleus. Only in the past five billion years or so could civilizations have safely arisen. The sun's relatively high metallicity probably gave us a head start. Therefore, the GHZ concept may provide at least a partial solution to the Fermi Paradox: complex life is so rare and isolated that we are effectively alone. To be sure, these implications apply only to complex life; simple organisms such as microbes could endure a much wider range of environments.

The broader universe looks even less inviting than our galaxy. About 80 percent of stars in the local universe reside in galaxies that are less luminous than the Milky Way. Because the average metallicity of a galaxy correlates with its luminosity, entire galaxies could be deficient in Earth-size planets. Another effect concerns the dynamics of stars in a galaxy. Like bees flying around a hive, stars in elliptical galaxies have randomized orbits and are therefore more likely to frequent their more dangerous central regions. In many ways, the Milky Way is unusually hospitable: a disk galaxy with orderly orbits, comparatively little dangerous activity and plenty of metals. It may not remain so for long. The Andromeda galaxy is predicted to have a close encounter with the Milky Way in about three billion years. That event will dislodge most stars in the disk from their regular orbits. It may also pour fresh fuel onto the Milky Way's central black hole and cause it to flare up, with possibly unhappy consequences for the inhabitants of Earth.

Douglas Adams, that great expositor of simple truths, famously summed up what he took to be the product of the past few centuries of progress in astronomy: "Far out in the uncharted backwaters of the unfashionable end of the western spiral arm of the Galaxy lies a small unregarded yellow sun." But as is often the case, fashionable is not the same as comfortable. We live in prime real estate.

More to Explore

Galactic Chemical Evolution: Implications for the Existence of Habitable Planets. Virginia Trimble in *Extraterrestrials: Where Are They?* Edited by M. H. Hart and B. Zuckerman. Cambridge University Press, 1995.

Worlds Without End: The Exploration of Planets Known and Unknown. John S. Lewis. Perseus Books, 1998.

Destiny or Chance: Our Solar System and Its Place in the Cosmos. Stuart R. Taylor. Cambridge University Press, 1998.

Rare Earth: Why Complex Life Is Uncommon in the Universe. Peter D. Ward and Donald Brownlee. Copernicus, 2000.

An Estimate of the Age Distribution of Terrestrial Planets in the Universe: Quantifying Metallicity as a Selection Effect. Charles H. Lineweaver in *Icarus*, Vol. 151, No. 2, pages 307–313; June 1, 2001. Preprint available at **astro-ph/0012399.**

The Galactic Habitable Zone: Galactic Chemical Evolution. Guillermo Gonzalez, Donald Brownlee and Peter D. Ward in *Icarus*, Vol. 152, No. 1, pages 185–200; July 1, 2001. Preprint available at **astro-ph/0103165.**

About the Authors

GUILLERMO GONZALEZ, DONALD BROWNLEE and *PETER D. WARD* share an interest in the habitability of planets—both because they happen to live on one and because habitability is an intellectual challenge that draws on nearly every field of astrophysics and geophysics. The three are members of the astrobiology program at the University of Washington, which NASA recently awarded an astrobiology grant. Gonzalez, currently at Iowa State University, earned his doctorate at Washington studying the compositions of highly evolved stars in globular clusters. Brownlee specializes in the study of comet dust and meteorites and is the principal investigator for the Stardust mission, which plans to return comet dust samples to Earth in January 2006. Ward, a paleontologist, studies global mass extinctions.

"The Paradox of the
4. Sun's Hot Corona

By Bhola N. Dwivedi and Kenneth J. H. Phillips

Like a boiling teakettle atop a cold stove, the sun's hot outer layers sit on the relatively cool surface. And now astronomers are figuring out why.

Relatively few people have witnessed a total eclipse of the sun—one of nature's most awesome spectacles. It was therefore a surprise for inhabitants of central Africa to see two total eclipses in quick succession, in June 2001 and December 2002. Thanks to favorable weather along the narrow track of totality across the earth, the 2001 event in particular captivated residents and visitors in Zambia's densely populated capital, Lusaka. One of us (Phillips), with colleagues from the U.K. and Poland, was also blessed with scientific equipment that worked perfectly on location at the University of Zambia. Other scientific teams captured valuable data from Angola and Zimbabwe. Most of us were trying to find yet more clues to one of the most enduring conundrums of the solar system: What is the mechanism that makes the sun's outer atmosphere, or corona, so hot?

The sun might appear to be a uniform sphere of gas, the essence of simplicity. In actuality it has well-defined layers that can loosely be compared to a planet's solid part and atmosphere. The solar radiation that we receive ultimately derives from nuclear reactions deep in the core. The energy gradually leaks out until it reaches the visible surface, known as the photosphere, and escapes into space. Above that surface is a tenuous atmosphere. The lowest part, the chromosphere, is usually visible only during total eclipses, as a bright red crescent. Beyond it is the pearly white corona, extending millions of kilometers. Further still, the corona becomes a stream of charged particles—the solar wind that blows through our solar system.

Journeying out from the sun's core, an imaginary observer first encounters temperatures of 15 million kelvins, high enough to generate the nuclear reactions that power the sun. Temperatures get progressively cooler en route to the photosphere, a mere 6,000 kelvins. But then an unexpected thing happens: the temperature gradient reverses. The chromosphere's temperature steadily rises to 10,000 kelvins, and going into the corona, the temperature jumps to one million kelvins. Parts of the corona associated with sunspots get even hotter. Considering that the energy must originate below the photosphere, how can this be? It is as if you got warmer the farther away you walked from a fireplace.

The first hints of this mystery emerged in the 19th century when eclipse observers detected spectral emission lines that no known element could account for. In the 1940s physicists associated two of these lines with iron atoms that had lost up to half their normal retinue of 26 electrons—a situation that requires extremely high temperatures. Later, instruments on rockets and satellites found that the sun emits copious x-rays and extreme ultraviolet radiation—as can be the case only if the coronal temperature is measured in megakelvins. Nor is this mystery confined to the sun: most sunlike stars appear to have x-ray-emitting atmospheres.

At last, however, a solution seems to be within our grasp. Astronomers have long implicated magnetic fields in the coronal heating; where those fields are strongest, the corona is hottest. Such fields can transport energy in a form other than heat, thereby sidestepping the usual thermodynamic restrictions. The energy must still be converted to heat, and researchers are testing two possible theories: small-scale magnetic field reconnections—the same process involved in solar flares—and magnetic waves. Important clues have come from complementary observations: spacecraft can observe at wavelengths inaccessible from the ground, while ground-based telescopes can gather reams of data unrestricted by the bandwidth of orbit-to-Earth radio links. The findings may be crucial to understanding how events on the sun affect the atmosphere of Earth [see "The Fury of Space Storms," by James L. Burch; *Scientific American*, April 2001].

The first high-resolution images of the corona came from the ultraviolet and x-ray telescopes on board Skylab, the American space station inhabited in 1973 and 1974. Pictures of active regions of the corona, located above sunspot groups, revealed complexes of

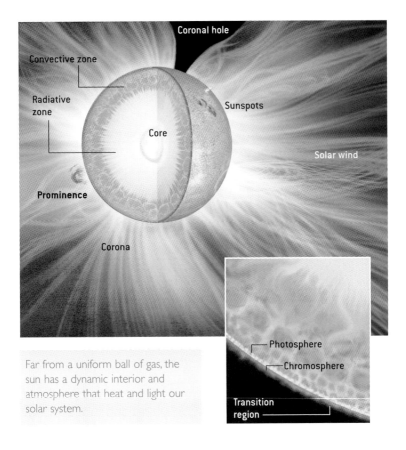

Coronal hole

Convective zone

Radiative zone

Sunspots

Core

Solar wind

Prominence

Corona

Far from a uniform ball of gas, the sun has a dynamic interior and atmosphere that heat and light our solar system.

Photosphere

Chromosphere

Transition region

loops that came and went in a matter of days. Much larger but more diffuse x-ray arches stretched over millions of kilometers, sometimes connecting sunspot groups. Away from active regions, in the "quiet" parts of the sun, ultraviolet emission had a honeycomb pattern related to the large convection granules in the photosphere. Near the solar poles and sometimes in equatorial locations were areas of very faint x-ray emission—the so-called coronal holes.

Connection to the Starry Dynamo

Each major solar spacecraft since Skylab has offered a distinct improvement in resolution. From 1991 to late 2001, the x-ray telescope on the Japanese Yohkoh spacecraft routinely imaged the sun's corona, tracking the evolution of loops and other features through one complete 11-year cycle of solar activity. The Solar and Heliospheric Observatory (SOHO), a joint European-American satellite launched in 1995, orbits a point 1.5 million kilometers from Earth on its sunward side, giving the spacecraft the advantage of an uninterrupted view of the sun [see "SOHO Reveals the Secrets of the Sun," by Kenneth R. Lang; *Scientific American*, March 1997]. One of its instruments, called the Large Angle and Spectroscopic Coronagraph (LASCO), observes in visible light using an opaque disk to mask out the main part of the sun. It has tracked large-scale coronal structures as they rotate with the rest of the sun (a period of about 27 days as seen from Earth). The images show huge bubbles of plasma known as coronal mass ejections, which move at up to 2,000 kilometers a second, erupting from the corona and occasionally colliding with Earth and other planets. Other SOHO instruments, such as the Extreme Ultraviolet Imaging Telescope, have greatly improved on Skylab's pictures.

The Transition Region and Coronal Explorer (TRACE) satellite, operated by the Stanford-Lockheed Institute for Space Research, went into a polar orbit around Earth in 1998. With unprecedented resolution, its ultraviolet telescope has revealed a vast wealth of detail. The active-region loops are now known to be threadlike features no more than a few hundred kilometers wide. Their incessant flickering and jouncing hint at the origin of the corona's heating mechanism.

The latest spacecraft dedicated to the sun is the Reuven Ramaty High Energy Solar Spectroscopic Imager (RHESSI), launched in 2002, which is providing images and spectra in the x-ray region of wavelengths less than four nanometers. Because solar activity has been high, much of its early attention was focused on intense flares, but as the solar minimum approaches, investigators will increasingly be interested in tiny microflares, a clue to the corona's heating mechanism.

The loops, arches and coronal holes trace out the sun's magnetic fields. The fields are thought to originate in the upper third of the solar interior, where energy is transported mostly by convection rather than radiation. A combination of convection currents and differential rotation—whereby low latitudes rotate slightly faster than higher latitudes—twist the fields to form ropelike or other tightly bound configurations that eventually emerge at the photosphere and into the solar atmosphere. Particularly intense fields are marked by sunspot groups and active regions.

For a century, astronomers have measured the magnetism of the photosphere using magnetographs, which observe the Zeeman effect: in the presence of a magnetic field, a spectral line can split into two or more lines with slightly different wavelengths and polarizations. But Zeeman observations for the corona have yet to be done. The spectral splitting is too small to be detected with present instruments, so astronomers have had to resort to mathematical extrapolations from the photospheric field. These predict that the magnetic field of the corona generally has a strength of about 10 gauss, 20 times Earth's magnetic field strength at its poles. In active regions, the field may reach 100 gauss.

Space Heaters

These fields are weak compared with those that can be produced with laboratory magnets, but they have a decisive influence in the solar corona. This is because the corona's temperature is so high that it is almost fully ionized: it is a plasma, made up not of neutral atoms but of electrons, protons and other atomic nuclei. Plasmas undergo a wide range of phenomena that neutral gases do not. The magnetic fields of the corona are strong enough to bind the charged particles to the field lines. Particles move in tight helical paths up and down these field lines like very small beads on very long strings. The limits on their motion explain the sharp boundaries of features such as coronal holes. Within the tenuous plasma, the magnetic pressure (proportional to the strength squared) exceeds the thermal pressure by a factor of at least 100.

One of the main reasons astronomers are confident that magnetic fields energize the corona is the clear relation between field strength and temperature. The bright loops of active regions, where there are extremely strong fields, have a temperature of about four million kelvins. But the giant arches of the quiet-sun corona, characterized by weak fields, have a temperature of about one million kelvins.

Until recently, however, ascribing coronal heating to magnetic fields ran into a serious problem. To convert field energy to heat energy, the fields must be able to diffuse through the plasma, which requires that the corona have a certain amount of electrical resistivity— in other words, that it not be a perfect conductor. A perfect conductor cannot sustain an electric field, because charged particles instantaneously reposition themselves to neutralize it. And if a plasma cannot sustain an electric field, it cannot move relative to the magnetic field (or vice versa), because to do so would induce an electric field. This is why astronomers talk about magnetic fields being "frozen" into plasmas.

This principle can be quantified by considering the time it takes a magnetic field to diffuse a certain distance through a plasma. The diffusion rate is inversely proportional to resistivity. Classical plasma physics assumes that electrical resistance arises from so-called Coulomb collisions: electrostatic forces from charged particles deflect the flow of electrons. If so, it should take about 10 million years to traverse a distance of 10,000 kilometers, a typical length of active-region loops.

Events in the corona—for example, flares, which may last for only a few minutes—far outpace that rate. Either the resistivity is unusually high or the diffusion distance is extremely small, or both. A distance as short as a few meters could occur in certain structures, accompanied by a steep magnetic gradient. But researchers have come to realize that the resistivity could be higher than they traditionally thought.

Raising the Mercury

Astronomers have two basic ideas for coronal heating. For years, they concentrated on heating by waves. Sound waves were a prime suspect, but in the late 1970s researchers established that sound waves emerging from the photosphere would dissipate in the chromosphere, leaving no energy for the corona itself. Suspicion turned to magnetic waves. Such waves might be purely magnetohydrodynamic (MHD)—so-called Alfvén waves—in which the field lines oscillate but the pressure does not. More likely, however, they share characteristics of both sound and Alfvén waves.

MHD theory combines two theories that are challenging in their own right—ordinary hydrodynamics and electromagnetism—although the broad outlines are clear. Plasma physicists recognize two kinds of MHD pressure waves, fast and slow mode, depending on the phase velocity relative to an Alfvén wave—around 2,000 kilometers a second in the corona. To traverse a typical active-region loop requires about five seconds for an Alfvén wave, less for a fast MHD wave, but at least half a minute for a slow wave. MHD waves are set into motion by convective perturbations in the photosphere and transported out into the corona via magnetic fields. They can then deposit their energy into the plasma if it has sufficient resistivity or viscosity.

A breakthrough occurred in 1998 when the TRACE spacecraft observed a powerful flare that triggered waves in nearby fine loops. The loops oscillated back and forth several times before settling down. The damping rate was millions of times as fast as classical theory predicts. This landmark observation of "coronal seismology" by Valery M. Nakariakov, then at the University of St. Andrews in Scotland, and his colleagues has shown that MHD waves could indeed deposit their energy into the corona.

An intriguing observation made with the ultraviolet coronagraph on the SOHO spacecraft has shown that highly ionized oxygen atoms have temperatures in coronal holes of more than 100 million kelvins, much higher than those of electrons and protons in the plasma. The temperatures also seem higher perpendicular to the magnetic field lines than parallel to them. Whether this is important for coronal heating remains to be seen.

Despite the plausibility of energy transport by waves, a second idea has been ascendant: that coronal heating is caused by very small, flarelike events. A flare is a sudden release of up to 10^{25} joules of energy in an active region of the sun. It is thought to be caused by reconnection of magnetic field lines, whereby oppositely directed lines cancel each other out, converting magnetic energy into heat. The process requires that the field lines be able to diffuse through the plasma.

A flare sends out a blast of x-rays and ultraviolet radiation. At the peak of the solar cycle (reached in 2000), several flares an hour may burst out across the sun. Spacecraft such as Yohkoh and SOHO have shown that much smaller but more frequent events take place not only in active regions but also in regions otherwise deemed quiet. These tiny events have about a millionth the energy of a full-blown flare and so are called microflares. They were first detected in 1980 by Robert P. Lin of the University of California at Berkeley and his colleagues with a balloon-borne hard x-ray detector. During the solar minimum in 1996, Yohkoh also recognized events with energy as small as 0.01 of a microflare.

Early results from the RHESSI measurements indicate more than 10 hard x-ray microflares an hour. In addition, RHESSI can produce images of microflares, which was not possible before. As solar activity declines, RHESSI should be able to locate and characterize very small flares.

Flares are not the only type of transient phenomena. X-ray and ultraviolet jets, representing columns of coronal material, are often seen spurting up from the lower corona at a few hundred kilometers a second. But tiny x-ray flares are of special interest because they reach the megakelvin temperatures required to heat the corona. Several researchers have attempted to extrapolate the microflare rates to even tinier nanoflares, to test an idea raised some years ago by Eugene Parker of the University of Chicago that numerous nanoflares occurring outside of active regions could account for the entire energy of the corona. Results remain confusing, but perhaps the combination of RHESSI, TRACE and SOHO data during the forthcoming minimum can provide an answer.

Which mechanism—waves or nanoflares— dominates? It depends on the photospheric motions that perturb the magnetic field. If these motions operate on timescales of half a minute or longer, they cannot trigger MHD waves. Instead they create narrow current sheets in which reconnections can occur. Very high resolution optical observations of bright filigree structures by the Swedish Vacuum Tower Telescope on La Palma in the Canary Islands— as well as SOHO and TRACE observations of a general, ever changing "magnetic carpet" on the surface of the sun—demonstrate that motions occur on a variety of timescales. Although the evidence now favors nanoflares for the bulk of coronal heating, waves may also play a role.

Fieldwork

It is unlikely, for example, that nanoflares have much effect in coronal holes. In these regions, the field lines open out into space rather than loop back to the sun, so a reconnection would accelerate plasma out into interplanetary space rather than heat it. Yet the corona in holes is still hot. Astronomers have scanned for signatures of wave motions, which may include periodic fluctuations in brightness or Doppler shift. The difficulty is that the MHD waves involved in heating probably have very short periods, perhaps just a few seconds. At present, spacecraft imaging is too sluggish to capture them.

For this reason, ground-based instruments remain important. A pioneer in this work has been Jay M. Pasachoff of Williams College. He and his students have used high-speed detectors and CCD cameras to look for modulations in the coronal light during eclipses. Analyses of his best results indicate oscillations with periods of one to two seconds. Serge Koutchmy of the Institute of Astrophysics in Paris, using a coronagraph, has found evidence of periods equal to 43, 80 and 300 seconds.

The search for those oscillations is what led Phillips and his colleagues to Bulgaria in 1999 and Zambia in 2001. Our instrument consists of a pair of fast-frame CCD cameras that observe both white light and the green spectral line produced by highly ionized iron. A tracking mirror, or heliostat, directs sunlight into a horizontal beam that passes into the instrument. At our observing sites, the 1999 eclipse totality lasted two minutes and 23 seconds, the 2001 totality three minutes and 38 seconds. Analyses of the 1999 eclipse by David A. Williams, now at University College London, reveal the possible presence of an MHD wave with fast-mode characteristics moving down a looplike structure. The CCD signal for this eclipse is admittedly weak, however, and Fourier analysis by Pawel Rudawy of the University of Wroclaw in Poland fails to find significant periodicities in the 1999 and 2001 data. We continue to try to determine if there are other, nonperiodic changes.

Insight into coronal heating has also come from observations of other stars. Current instruments cannot see surface features of these stars directly, but spectroscopy can deduce the presence of starspots, and ultraviolet and x-ray observations can reveal coronae and flares, which are often much more powerful than their solar counterparts. High-resolution spectra from the Extreme Ultraviolet Explorer and the latest x-ray satellites, Chandra and XMM-Newton, can probe temperature and density. For example, Capella—a stellar system consisting of two giant stars—has photospheric temperatures like the sun's but coronal temperatures that are six times higher. The intensities of individual spectral lines indicate a plasma density of about 100 times that of the solar corona. This high density implies that Capella's coronae are much smaller than the sun's, stretching out a tenth or less of a stellar diameter. Apparently, the distribution of the magnetic field differs from star to star. For some stars, tightly orbiting planets might even play a role.

Even as one corona mystery begins to yield to our concerted efforts, additional ones appear. The sun and other stars, with their complex layering, magnetic fields and effervescent dynamism, still manage to defy our understanding. In an age of such exotica as black holes and dark matter, even something that seems mundane can retain its allure.

More to Explore

Guide to the Sun. Kenneth J. H. Phillips. Cambridge University Press, 1992.

The Solar Corona above Polar Coronal Holes as Seen by Sumer on SOHO. Klaus Wilhelm et al. in *Astrophysical Journal*, Vol. 500, No. 2, pages 1023–1038; June 20, 1998.

Today's Science of the Sun, Parts 1 and 2. Carolus J. Schrijver and Alan M. Title in *Sky & Telescope*, Vol. 101, No. 2, pages 34–39; February 2001; and No. 3, pages 34–40; March 2001.

Glorious Eclipses: Their Past, Present and Future. Serge Brunier and Jean-Pierre Luminet. Cambridge University Press, 2001.

Probing the Sun's Hot Corona. K.J.H. Phillips and B. N. Dwivedi in *Dynamic Sun*. Edited by B. N. Dwivedi. Cambridge University Press, 2003.

About the Authors

BHOLA N. DWIVEDI and *KENNETH J. H. PHILLIPS* began collaborating on solar physics a decade ago. Dwivedi teaches physics at Banaras Hindu University in Varanasi, India. He has been working with SUMER, an ultraviolet telescope on the SOHO spacecraft, for more than 10 years; the Max Planck Institute for Aeronomy near Hannover, Germany, recently awarded him one of its highest honors, the Gold Pin. As a boy, Dwivedi studied by the light of a homemade burner and became the first person in his village ever to attend college. Phillips recently left the Rutherford Appleton Laboratory in England to become a senior research associate in the Reuven Ramaty High Energy Solar Spectroscopic Imager group at the NASA Goddard Space Flight Center in Greenbelt, Md. He has worked with x-ray and ultraviolet instruments on numerous spacecraft—including OSO-4, SolarMax, IUE, Yohkoh, Chandra and SOHO—and has observed three solar eclipses using CCD cameras.

"The Gas
5. between the Stars"

by Ronald J. Reynolds

Filled with colossal fountains of hot gas and vast bubbles blown by exploding stars, the interstellar medium is far more interesting than scientists once thought.

We often think of the moon as a place, but in fact it is a hundred million places, an archipelago of solitude. You could go from 100 degrees below zero to 100 degrees above with a small step. You could yell in your friend's ear and he would never hear you. Without an atmosphere to transmit heat or sound, each patch of the moon is an island in an unnavigable sea.

The atmosphere of a planet is what binds its surface into a unified whole. It lets conditions such as temperature vary smoothly. More dramatically, events such as the impact of an asteroid, the eruption of a volcano and the emission of gas from a factory's chimney can have effects that reach far beyond the spots where they took place. Local phenomena can have global consequences. This characteristic of atmospheres has begun to capture the interest of astronomers who study the Milky Way galaxy.

For many years, we have known that an extremely thin atmosphere called the interstellar medium envelops our galaxy and threads the space between its billions of stars. Until fairly recently, the medium seemed a cold, static reservoir of gas quietly waiting to condense into stars. You barely even notice it when looking up into the starry sky. Now we recognize the medium as a tempestuous mixture with an extreme diversity of density, temperature and ionization. Supernova explosions blow giant bubbles; fountains and chimneys may arch above the spiral disk; and clouds could be falling in from beyond the disk. These and other processes interconnect far-flung reaches of our galaxy much as atmospheric phenomena convey disturbances from one side of Earth to the other.

In fact, telescopes on the ground and in space are showing the galaxy's atmosphere to be as complex as any planet's. Held by the combined gravitational pull of the stars and other matter, permeated by starlight, energetic particles and a magnetic field, the interstellar medium is continuously stirred, heated, recycled and transformed. Like any atmosphere, it has its highest density and pressure at the "bottom," in this case the plane that defines the middle of the galaxy, where the pressure must balance the weight of the medium from "above." Dense concentrations of gas—clouds—form near the midplane, and from the densest subcondensations, stars precipitate.

When stars exhaust their nuclear fuel and die, those that are at least as massive as the sun expel much of their matter back into the interstellar medium. Thus, as the galaxy ages, each generation of stars pollutes the medium with heavy elements. As in the water cycle on Earth, precipitation is followed by "evaporation," so that material can be recycled over and over again.

Up in the Air

Thinking of the interstellar medium as a true atmosphere brings unity to some of the most pressing problems in astrophysics. First and foremost is star formation. Although astronomers have known the basic principles for decades, they still do not grasp exactly what determines when and at what rate stars precipitate from the interstellar medium. Theorists used to explain the creation of stars only in terms of the local conditions within an isolated gas cloud. Now they are considering conditions in the galaxy as a whole.

Not only do these conditions influence star formation, they are influenced by it. What one generation of stars does determines the environment in which subsequent generations are born, live and die. Understanding this feedback—the sway of stars, especially the hottest, rarest, most massive stars, over the large-scale properties of the interstellar medium—is another of the great challenges for researchers. Feedback can be both positive and negative. On the one hand, massive stars can heat and ionize the medium and cause it to bulge out from the midplane. This expansion increases the ambient pressure, compressing the clouds and perhaps triggering their collapse into a new generation of stars. On the other hand, the heating and ionization can also agitate clouds, inhibiting the birth of new stars. When the largest stars blow up, they can even destroy the clouds that gave them birth. In fact, negative feedback could explain why the gravitational collapse of clouds into stars is so inefficient. Typically only a few percent of a cloud's mass becomes stars.

A third conundrum is that star formation often occurs in sporadic but intense bursts. In the Milky Way the competing feedback effects almost balance out, so that stars form at an unhurried pace—just 10 per year on average. In some galaxies, however, such as the "exploding galaxy" M82, positive feedback has gained the upper hand. Starting 20 million to 50 million years ago, star formation in the central parts of M82 began running out of control, proceeding 10 times faster than before. Our galaxy, too, may have had sporadic bursts. How these starbursts occur and what turns them off must be tied to the complex relation between stars and the tenuous atmosphere from which they precipitate.

Finally, astronomers debate how quickly the atmospheric activity is petering out. The majority of stars—those less massive than the sun, which live tens or even hundreds of billions of years—do not contribute to the feedback loops. More and more of the interstellar gas is being locked up into very long lived stars. Eventually all the spare gas in our Milky Way may be exhausted, leaving only stellar dregs behind. How soon this will happen depends on whether the Milky Way is a closed box. Recent observations suggest that the galaxy is still an open system, both gaining and losing mass to its cosmic surroundings. High-velocity clouds of relatively unpolluted hydrogen appear to be raining down from intergalactic space, rejuvenating our galaxy. Meanwhile the galaxy may be shedding gas in the form of a high-speed wind from its outer atmosphere, much as the sun slowly sheds mass in the solar wind.

Hot and Cold Running Hydrogen

To tackle these problems, those of us who study the interstellar medium have first had to identify its diverse components. Astronomers carried out the initial step, an analysis of its elemental composition, in the 1950s and 1960s using the spectra of light emitted by bright nebulae, such as the Orion Nebula. In terms of the number of atomic nuclei, hydrogen constitutes 90 percent, helium about 10 percent, and everything else—from lithium to uranium—just a trace, about 0.1 percent.

Because hydrogen is so dominant, the structure of the galaxy's atmosphere depends mainly on what forms the hydrogen takes. Early observations were sensitive primarily to cooler, neutral components. The primary marker of interstellar material is the most famous spectral line of astronomy: the 1,420-megahertz (21-centimeter) line emitted by neutral hydrogen atoms, denoted by astronomers as H I. Beginning in the 1950s, radio astronomers mapped out the distribution of H I within the galaxy. It resides in lumps and filaments with densities of 10 to 100 atoms per cubic centimeter and temperatures near 100 kelvins, embedded in a more diffuse, thinner (roughly 0.1 atom per cubic centimeter) and warmer (a few thousand kelvins) phase. Most of the H I is close to the galactic midplane, forming a gaseous disk about 300 parsecs (1,000 light-years) thick, roughly half the thickness of the main stellar disk you see when you notice the Milky Way in the night sky.

Hydrogen can also come in a molecular form (H_2), which is extremely difficult to detect directly. Much of the information about it has been inferred from high-frequency radio observations of the trace molecule carbon monoxide. Where carbon monoxide exists, so should molecular hydrogen. The molecules appear to be confined to the densest and coldest clouds—the places where starlight, which breaks molecules into their constituent atoms, cannot penetrate. These dense clouds, which are active sites of star formation, are found in a thin layer (100 parsecs thick) at the very bottom of the galactic atmosphere.

Until very recently, hydrogen molecules were seen directly only in places where they were being destroyed—that is, converted to atomic hydrogen—by a nearby star's ultraviolet radiation or wind of outflowing particles. In these environments, H_2 glows at an infrared wavelength of about 2.2 microns. In the past few years, however, orbiting spectrographs, such as the shuttle-based platform called ORFEUS-SPAS and the new Far Ultraviolet Spectroscopic Explorer (FUSE) satellite, have sought molecular hydrogen at ultraviolet wavelengths near 0.1 micron. These instruments look for hydrogen that is backlit by distant stars and quasars: the H_2 leaves telltale absorption lines in the ultraviolet spectra of those objects. The advantage of this approach is that it can detect molecular hydrogen in quiescent regions of the galaxy, far from any star.

To general astonishment, two teams, led respectively by Philipp Richter of the University of Wisconsin and Wolfgang Gringel of the University of Tübingen in Germany, have discovered H_2 not just in the usual places—the high-density clouds located within the galactic disk—but also in low-density areas far outside the disk. This is a bit of a mystery, because high densities are needed to shield the molecules from the ravages of starlight. Perhaps a population of cool clouds extends much farther from the midplane than previously believed.

A third form of hydrogen is a plasma of hydrogen ions. Astronomers used to assume that ionized hydrogen was confined to a few small, isolated locations—the glowing nebulae near luminous stars and the wispy remnants left over from supernovae. Advances in detection technology and the advent of space astronomy have changed that. Two new components of our galaxy's atmosphere have come into view: hot (10^6 kelvins) and warm (10^4 kelvins) ionized hydrogen (H II).

Like the recently detected hydrogen molecules, these H II phases stretch far above the cold H I cloud layer, forming a thick gaseous "halo" around the entire galaxy. "Interstellar" no longer seems an appropriate description for these outermost parts of our galaxy's atmosphere. The hotter phase may extend thousands of parsecs from the midplane and thin out to a density near 10^{-3} ion per cubic centimeter. It is our galaxy's corona, analogous to the extended hot atmosphere of our sun. As in the case of the solar corona, the mere existence of the galactic corona implies an unconventional source of energy to maintain the high temperatures. Supernova shocks and fast stellar winds appear to do the trick. Coexisting with the hot plasma is the warm plasma, which is powered by extreme ultraviolet radiation. The weight of these extended layers increases the gas pressure at the midplane, with significant effects on star formation. Other galaxies appear to have coronas as well. The Chandra X-ray Observatory has recently seen one around the galaxy NGC 4631.

Blowing Bubbles

Having identified these new, more energetic phases of the medium, astronomers have turned to the question of how the diverse components behave and interrelate.

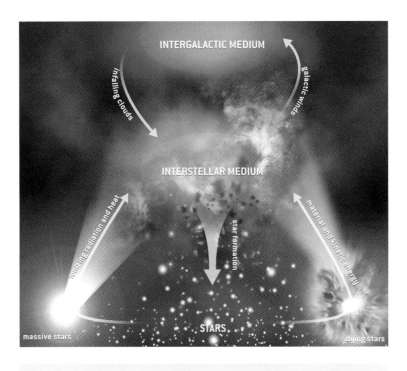

Recycling of gas by the galaxy is analogous to the water cycle on Earth. The interstellar medium plays the part of the atmosphere. Stars "precipitate" out and then "evaporate" back; the more massive ones energize and stir the medium. And just as Earth loses material to (and gains material from) interplanetary space, so too does the galaxy exchange material with intergalactic space.

Not only does the interstellar medium cycle through stars, it changes from H_2 to H I to H II and from cold to hot and back again. Massive stars are the only known source of energy powerful enough to account for all this activity. A study by Ralf-Jürgen Dettmar of the University of Bochum in Germany found that galaxies with a larger-than-average massive star population seem to have atmospheres that are more extended or puffed up. How the stars wield power over an entire galaxy is somewhat unclear, but astronomers generally pin the blame on the creation of hot ionized gas.

This gas appears to be produced by the high-velocity (100 to 200 kilometers per second) shock waves that expand into the interstellar medium following a supernova. Depending on the density of the gas and strength of the magnetic field in the ambient medium, the spherically expanding shock may clear out a cavity 50 to 100 parsecs in radius—a giant bubble.

In doing so, the shock accelerates a small fraction of the ions and electrons to near light speed. Known as cosmic rays, these fleet-footed particles are one way that stellar death feeds back (both positively and negatively) into stellar birth. Cosmic rays raise the pressure of the interstellar medium; higher pressures, in turn, compress the dense molecular clouds and increase the chance that they will collapse into stars. By ionizing some of the hydrogen, the cosmic rays also drive chemical reactions that synthesize complex molecules, some of which are the building blocks of life as we know it. And because the ions attach themselves to magnetic field lines, they trap the field within the clouds, which slows the rate of cloud collapse into stars.

If hot bubbles are created frequently enough, they could interconnect in a vast froth. This idea was first advanced in the 1970s by Barham Smith and Donald

Cox of the University of Wisconsin–Madison. A couple of years later Christopher F. McKee of the University of California at Berkeley and Jeremiah P. Ostriker of Princeton University argued that the hot phase should occupy 55 to 75 percent of interstellar space. Cooler neutral phases would be confined to isolated clouds within this ionized matrix—essentially the inverse of the traditional picture, in which the neutral gas dominates and the ionized gas is confined to small pockets.

Recent observations seem to support this upending of conventional wisdom. The nearby spiral galaxy M101, for example, has a circular disk of atomic hydrogen gas riddled with holes—presumably blown by massive stars. The interstellar medium of another galaxy, seven billion light-years distant, also looks like Swiss cheese. But the amount of hot gas and its influence on the structure of galactic atmospheres still occasion much debate.

Chimneys and Fountains

The sun itself appears to be located within a hot bubble, which has revealed itself in x-rays emitted by highly ionized trace ions such as oxygen. Called the Local Bubble, this region of hot gas was apparently created by a nearby supernova about one million years ago.

An even more spectacular example lies 450 parsecs from the sun in the direction of the constellations Orion and Eridanus. It was the subject of a recent study by Carl Heiles of the University of California at Berkeley and his colleagues. The Orion-Eridanus Bubble was formed by a star cluster in the constellation Orion. The cluster is of an elite type called an OB association—a bundle of the hottest and most massive stars, the O- and B-type stars, which are 20 to 60 times heavier than the sun (a G-type star) and 103 to 105 times brighter. The spectacular deaths of these short-lived stars in supernovae over the past 10 million years have swept the ambient gas into a shell-like skin around the outer boundary of the bubble. In visible light the shell appears as a faint lacework of ionized loops and filaments. The million-degree gas that fills its interior gives off a diffuse glow of x-rays.

The entire area is a veritable thunderstorm of star formation, with no sign of letting up. Stars continue to precipitate from the giant molecular cloud out of which the OB association emerged. One of the newest O stars, theta[1] C Orionis, is ionizing a small piece of the cloud—producing the Orion Nebula. In time, however, supernovae and ionizing radiation will completely disrupt the molecular cloud and dissociate its molecules. The molecular hydrogen will turn back into atomic and ionized hydrogen, and star formation will cease. Because the violent conversion process will increase the pressure in the interstellar medium, the demise of this molecular cloud may mean the birth of stars else-where in the galaxy.

Galactic bubbles should buoyantly lift off from the galactic midplane, like a thermal rising above the heated ground on Earth. Numerical calculations, such as those recently made by Mordecai-Mark MacLow of the American Museum of Natural History in New York City and his colleagues, suggest that bubbles can ascend all the way up into the halo of the galaxy. The result is a cosmic chimney through which hot gas spewed by supernovae near the midplane can vent to the galaxy's upper atmosphere. There the gas will cool and rain back onto the galactic disk. In this case, the superbubble and chimney become a galactic-scale fountain.

Such fountains could perhaps be the source of the hot galactic corona and even the galaxy's magnetic field. According to calculations by Katia M. Ferrière of the Midi-Pyrénées Observatory in France, the combination of the updraft and the rotation of the galactic disk would act as a dynamo, much as motions deep inside the sun and Earth generate magnetic fields.

To be sure, observers have yet to prove the pervasive nature of the hot phase or the presence of fountains. The Orion-Eridanus bubble extends 400 parsecs from the midplane, and a similar superbubble in Cassiopeia rises 230 parsecs, but both have another 1,000 to 2,000 parsecs to go to reach the galactic corona. Magnetic fields and cooler, denser ionized gas could make it difficult or impossible for superbubbles to break out into the halo. But then, where did the hot corona come from? No plausible alternative is known.

Getting Warm

The warm (10^4 kelvins) plasma is as mysterious as its hot relative. Indeed, in the traditional picture of the interstellar medium, the widespread presence of warm ionized gas is simply impossible. Such gas should be limited to very small regions of space—the emission nebulae, such as the Orion Nebula, that immediately surround ultramassive stars. These stars account for only one star in five million, and most of the interstellar gas (the atomic and molecular hydrogen) is opaque to their photons. So the bulk of the galaxy should be unaffected.

Yet warm ionized gas is spread throughout interstellar space. One recent survey, known as WHAM, finds it even in the galactic halo, very far from the nearest O stars. Ionized gas is similarly widespread in other galaxies. This is a huge mystery. How did the ionizing photons manage to stray so far from their stars?

Bubbles may be the answer. If supernovae have hollowed out significant parts of the interstellar medium, ionizing photons may be able to travel large distances before being absorbed by neutral hydrogen. The Orion OB association provides an excellent example of how this could work. The O stars sit in an immense cavity carved out by earlier supernovae. Their photons now travel freely across the cavity, striking the distant bubble wall and making it glow. If galactic fountains or chimneys do indeed stretch up into the galactic halo, they could explain not only the hot corona but also the pervasiveness of warm ionized gas.

A new WHAM image of the Cassiopeia superbubble reveals a possible clue: a loop of warm gas arching far above the bubble, some 1,200 parsecs from the midplane. The outline of this loop bears a loose resemblance to a chimney, except that it has not (yet) broken out into the Milky Way's outer halo. The amount of energy required to produce this gigantic structure is enormous—more than that available from the stars in the cluster that formed the bubble. Moreover, the time required to create it is 10 times the age of the cluster. So the loop may be a multigenerational project, created by a series of distinct bursts of star formation predating the cluster we see today. Each burst reenergized and expanded the bubble created by the preceding burst.

Round and Round

That large regions of the galaxy can be influenced by the formation of massive stars in a few localized regions seems to require that star formation somehow be coordinated over long periods of time. It may all begin with a single O-type star or a cluster of such stars in a giant molecular cloud. The stellar radiation, winds and explosions carve a modest cavity out of the surrounding interstellar medium. In the process the parent cloud is probably destroyed. Perchance this disturbance triggers star formation in a nearby cloud, and so on, until the interstellar medium in this corner of the galaxy begins to resemble Swiss cheese. The bubbles then begin to overlap, coalescing into a superbubble. The energy from more and more O-type stars feeds this expanding superbubble until its natural buoyancy stretches it from the midplane up toward the halo, forming a chimney.

The superbubble is now a pathway for hot interior gas to spread into the upper reaches of the galactic atmosphere, producing a widespread corona. Now, far from its source of energy, the coronal gas slowly begins to cool and condense into clouds. These clouds fall back to the galaxy's midplane, completing the fountainlike cycle and replenishing the galactic disk with cool clouds from which star formation may begin anew.

Even though the principal components and processes of our galaxy's atmosphere seem to have been identified, the details remain uncertain. Progress will be made as astronomers continue to study how the medium is cycled through stars, through the different phases of the medium, and between the disk and the halo. Observations of other galaxies give astronomers a bird's-eye view of the interstellar goings-on.

Some crucial pieces could well be missing. For example, are stars really the main source of power for the interstellar medium? The loop above the Cassiopeia superbubble looks uncomfortably similar to the prominences that arch above the surface of the sun. Those prominences owe much to the magnetic field in the solar atmosphere. Could it be that magnetic activity dominates our galaxy's atmosphere, too? If so, the analogy between galactic atmospheres and their stellar and planetary counterparts may be even more apt than we think.

More to Explore

Ionizing the Galaxy. Ronald J. Reynolds in *Science*, Vol. 277, pages 1446–1447; September 5, 1997.

Far Ultraviolet Spectroscopic Explorer Observations of O VI Absorption in the Galactic Halo. Blair D. Savage et al. in *Astrophysical Journal Letters*, Vol. 538, No. 1, pages L27–L30; July 20, 2000. Preprint available at **arXiv.org/abs/astro-ph/0005045**.

Gas in Galaxies. Joss Bland-Hawthorn and Ronald J. Reynolds in *Encyclopaedia of Astronomy & Astrophysics*. MacMillan and Institute of Physics Publishing, 2000. Preprint available at **arXiv.org/abs/astro-ph/0006058**.

Detection of a Large Arc of Ionized Hydrogen Far Above the CAS OB6 Association: A Superbubble Blowout into the Galactic Halo? Ronald J. Reynolds, N. C. Sterling and L. Matthew Haffner in *Astrophysical Journal Letters*, Vol. 558, No. 2, pages L101–L104; September 10, 2001. Preprint available at **arXiv.org/abs/astro-ph/0108046**.

The Interstellar Environment of Our Galaxy. K. M. Ferrière in *Reviews of Modern Physics*, Vol. 73, No. 4 (in press). Preprint available at **arXiv.org/abs/astro-ph/0106359**.

About the Author

RONALD J. REYNOLDS bought a 4.25-inch reflecting telescope in sixth grade and used it to take pictures of the moon. But it wasn't until he started his Ph.D. in physics that he took his first astronomy course and began to consider a career in the subject. Today Reynolds is an astronomy professor at the University of Wisconsin–Madison. He has designed and built high-sensitivity spectrometers to study warm ionized gas in the Milky Way galaxy. He is principal investigator for the Wisconsin H-Alpha Mapper, which spent two years mapping hydrogen over the entire northern sky.

"The Secrets
6. of Stardust"

By J. Mayo Greenberg

Tiny grains of dust floating in interstellar space have radically altered the history of our galaxy.

Look up at the sky on any clear night, and you will see dark patches in the Milky Way, the fuzzy band of light generated by the billions of stars in our galaxy. Sir William Herschel, the 18th-century English astronomer, thought the patches were literally "holes in the sky," empty spaces in the heavens. In the early 20th century, astronomers discovered that the dark patches are actually tremendous clouds of dust that obscure the light of the stars behind them. The individual particles of cosmic dust are minute: less than one hundredth the size of the particles that you sweep up with a dust mop. And yet these tiny dust grains have greatly influenced the evolution of our galaxy and the formation of stars throughout the universe.

Until the 1950s, many astronomers considered the dust a nuisance because it kept them from seeing distant stars. In recent years, however, researchers have focused on the interstellar dust grains, measuring their distribution and chemical composition using ground- and space-based telescopes. The wealth of new data has made it possible to develop a plausible hypothesis of how this stardust has evolved. Aigen Li, my former student and now a postdoc at Princeton University, and I have devised a theory that we call the unified dust model. Although other researchers have advocated alternative theories, we believe our model provides the best explanation of the new observations.

In the Milky Way, dust clouds are concentrated in the galactic plane, particularly along the inner edges of the galaxy's spiral arms. These areas appear extremely patchy, with dense clusters of stars interspersed among the dust clouds. The clouds reduce the intensity of starlight more strongly in the blue and ultraviolet parts of the spectrum than in the red and infrared parts. Therefore, when astronomers see stars through the dust, they always appear redder than they really are. Similarly, our sun looks redder near the horizon because dust and gas in the Earth's atmosphere scatter its light.

It turns out that the largest interstellar dust motes are about the same size as the particles in cigarette smoke. The extinction curve for interstellar dust, which portrays the reduction of light intensity at each wave-length, shows that there must be three kinds of dust grains [see "Our Dusty Galaxy" box]. The particles that block light in the visible spectrum are elongated grains nearly 0.2 micron (two ten-millionths of a meter) wide and about twice as long. They account for about 80 percent of the total mass of interstellar dust. Each grain contains a rocky core surrounded by a mantle of organic materials and ice. A "hump" in the ultraviolet part of the extinction curve indicates the presence of smaller particles (with a diameter of about 0.005 micron), which make up about 10 percent of the total dust mass. These grains are most likely amorphous carbonaceous solids that probably contain some hydrogen but little or no nitrogen or oxygen. And an even smaller kind of particle, only about 0.002 micron across, is responsible for blocking light in the far ultraviolet region. These specks, which constitute the remaining 10 percent of the dust mass, are believed to be large molecules similar to the polycyclic aromatic hydrocarbons (PAHs) emitted in automobile exhaust.

Because the dust grains are usually far from stars, they are extremely cold, reaching temperatures as low as –268 degrees Celsius, or just five degrees above absolute zero. In the 1940s the brilliant Dutch astronomer Henk van de Hulst (my dear friend and mentor) theorized that some of the atoms known to exist in interstellar space—hydrogen, oxygen, carbon and nitrogen—would adhere to the cold surfaces of the dust grains and form mantles of frozen water, methane and ammonia. I later dubbed this theory the "dirty ice" model.

It was not until the early 1970s, however, that astronomers found strong evidence for the theory. While studying the infrared spectra of starlight passing through interstellar dust clouds, researchers detected the distinctive absorption lines of silicates—compounds of silicon, magnesium and iron. Silicates make up the rocky cores of the dust grains. At about the same time, scientists also observed the absorption line of frozen water in the infrared spectra. Later observations indicated the presence of carbon monoxide, carbon dioxide, formaldehyde and many other compounds as well. These substances are classified as volatiles—they freeze on contact with the cold dust grains but evaporate if the dust is warmed up. In contrast, the substances in the cores of the dust grains are called refractories—they remain solid at higher temperatures.

Interstellar dust constitutes about one thousandth of the Milky Way's mass—an amount probably hundreds of times more than the total mass of all the galaxy's planets. The particles are sparsely distributed: on average, you will find only one dust grain in every million cubic meters of space. But as starlight travels through thousands of light-years of dust, even this wispy distribution can effectively dim the radiation. So the question arises: How did our galaxy get so dusty?

From Dust to Dust

In the first era of the universe, some 15 billion years ago, there was no dust. Like all the other early galaxies, the Milky Way consisted solely of hydrogen, helium and a smattering of other light elements created in the big bang. During this period, only extremely massive clouds of hydrogen and helium could contract into stars, because a truly enormous amount of gravitational attraction was needed to overcome the pressure caused by the gases' thermodynamic motion. Thus, our galaxy was dominated by gigantic O- and B-type stars, which exploded in supernovae only a few million years after their birth. The first dust was produced by these supernovae; astronomers see evidence of it in the early galaxies observed by far-infrared telescopes that view submillimeter wavelengths. But this dust did not last long in the interstellar medium—the shock waves from subsequent supernovae destroyed the particles soon after they were created.

After about five billion years, though, the storm of supernovae subsided and the stars that were not quite so massive entered the red-giant phase of their lifetimes. As these stars cooled and expanded, rocky silicate particles formed in the stars' atmospheres and were blown into interstellar space. Some of these silicate particles entered the clouds of molecular gas that were constantly moving among the stars. In the low temperatures inside the clouds, every atom or molecule that encountered a silicate grain immediately froze on its surface, just as drops of water vapor freeze on a cold windowpane. In this way, an icy mantle grew on each of the silicate cores.

As dust concentrated in the molecular clouds, the density of the grains rose tens of thousands of times higher than the density outside the clouds. The dust became thick enough to block nearly all radiation from entering the clouds, lowering the temperature of the gas still further. Because the clouds were cooler than before, not as much mass was needed to overcome the gas pressure. Smaller gas clouds, then, could contract, and smaller stars such as our own sun could be born. By easing the constraints on star formation, the presence of dust radically changed the makeup of the Milky Way.

What is more, our galaxy's dust is continually recycled. When a dense cloud of gas and dust contracts to form a star, the dust grains closest to the star-forming region evaporate. (The silicon and other elements from these dust grains either become part of the star or later

Our Dusty Galaxy

Dust clouds such as those in the Rosette Nebula are stellar nurseries. The dust grains block radiation within the gaseous clouds, making it easier for them to collapse and form stars. In the process, most of the dust is blown away to emptier regions of space. Measurements of the extinction of starlight passing through these sparse regions (below) indicate the presence of three types of dust particles: core-mantle grains, amorphous carbonaceous solids, and large molecules similar to polycyclic aromatic hydrocarbons (PAHs). The core-mantle grains can also account for the starlight polarization at all wavelengths.

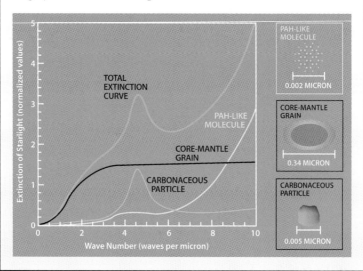

condense to form rocky planets and asteroids.) But the great majority of the dust is blown away into diffuse clouds—regions of space where the gas is much less dense. In this harsher environment, the ice mantles on the dust grains not only cease to grow but are destroyed or eroded away by ultraviolet radiation, particle collisions and supernova shock fronts. The grains are not reduced to their silicate cores, however. Underneath the outer mantle of ice is an inner mantle consisting of complex organic materials.

Three decades ago I proposed the existence of this organic mantle because I determined that silicates alone could not account for the amount of light extinction caused by the dust in diffuse clouds. I hypothesized that the layer of carbon-rich material on the dust grain is produced by chemical reactions in the ice mantle that begin when the grain is still in the dense cloud of molecular gas. According to my theory, when energetic ultraviolet photons strike the ice mantle, they break the water, methane and ammonia molecules into free radicals, which then recombine to form organic molecules such as formaldehyde. Continued ultraviolet irradiation eventually gives rise to more complex compounds called first-generation organics. They remain as a residue on the silicate core even after the dust grain leaves the molecular cloud and the ice mantle is destroyed. In fact, the organic mantle helps to shield the silicate core from supernova shocks, preserving the dust grain until it returns to the shelter of another dense gas cloud.

Yellow and Brown Stuff

To test this theory, I began laboratory experiments that simulated the conditions affecting the ice mantles. The work started at the State University of New York at Albany in 1970 and continued at the University of Leiden in the Netherlands in 1975. Our research group subjected various ice mixtures to ultraviolet radiation at a temperature of −263 degrees C, then warmed the mixtures. The result was a yellow-colored residue that we called, appropriately enough, "yellow stuff." The residue contained glycerol, glyceramide, several amino acids (including glycine, serine and alanine), and a host of other complex molecules.

At about the same time, astronomers had detected evidence of complex organic compounds in the dust of diffuse clouds by measuring the absorption of starlight passing through them. Our lab results did not precisely duplicate the absorption lines in the infrared spectra, but we should not have been surprised by this discrepancy. In the exposed environment of diffuse clouds the dust grains are subjected to ultraviolet radiation 10,000 times more intense than that in molecular clouds. This radiation transforms the material in the inner mantles to second-generation organics. The extra amount of ultraviolet processing was difficult to reproduce in the laboratory.

Fortunately, opportunity knocked at the lab door. In the late 1980s Gerda Horneck of DLR, Germany's space agency, invited us to use a satellite platform called the Exobiology Radiation Assembly, which was originally designed for exposing biological specimens to long-term ultraviolet radiation. It was also ideally suited for the ultraviolet processing of our "yellow stuff." Our research group, which included Menno de Groot, Celia Mendoza-Gómez, Willem Schutte and Peter Weber, prepared the organic residues and sent them into orbit in the European Retrievable Carrier (EURECA) satellite, which was launched by the space shuttle in 1992.

After a year (but only four months of actual exposure to solar ultraviolet radiation), the shuttle retrieved the satellite, and the samples were returned to us. What went up yellow came back brown. The color change indicated that the material had become richer in carbon. When we studied the "brown stuff" with an infrared spectrometer, we found the exact same pattern of absorption lines that had been detected in the infrared observations of interstellar dust. Even though the radiation exposure for the sample was only about one tenth the maximum exposure for a dust grain in a diffuse cloud, our sample closely approximated the organic refractory materials in cosmic dust.

These experiments laid the groundwork for the unified dust model that Aigen Li and I constructed. The theory postulates that the two smaller types of interstellar dust grains—the amorphous carbonaceous particles and the molecules similar to PAHs—arise from the ultraviolet processing of the organic materials in the larger core-mantle dust grains. We brought our sample of "brown stuff" to Seb Gillette of Stanford University for analysis using the sophisticated mass spectrometry techniques developed by Stanford chemist Richard Zare. Gillette found that the sample was extremely rich in PAHs. The unified dust model suggests that the chemical processing in the core-mantle grains can account for nearly all the small carbonaceous particles and PAH-like molecules in interstellar dust. In the diffuse gas clouds the small particles break off from the organic mantles when supernova shocks shatter the larger dust grains [see "The Dust Cycle" box]. Each core-mantle particle generates a swarm of hundreds of thousands of the minuscule grains.

Eventually the entire ensemble of dust is captured by a dense molecular cloud. Inside the cloud, collisions between the dust particles and the atoms and molecules of gas become more frequent. After a million years or so, the larger dust grains accrete an ice mantle dominated by frozen water and carbon monoxide. Observations of the dust in very dense clouds around stars have indicated the presence of these compounds, along with smaller amounts of carbon dioxide, formaldehyde and ammonia. Although no one has directly observed what happens to the carbonaceous particles and PAH-like molecules in a molecular cloud, it is inevitable that they will also accrete on the larger dust grains and be taken up in the ice mantles. The organic molecules are then reprocessed by ultraviolet radiation, and the cycle begins anew.

Other scientists have proposed alternative models that can explain the extinction effects of interstellar dust without the need for organic mantles on the larger dust grains. For example, John S. Mathis of the

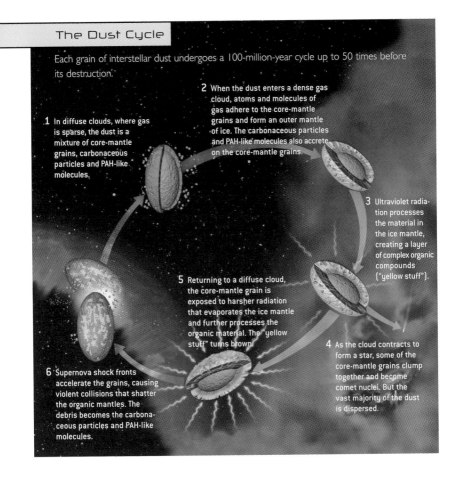

The Dust Cycle

Each grain of interstellar dust undergoes a 100-million-year cycle up to 50 times before its destruction.

1 In diffuse clouds, where gas is sparse, the dust is a mixture of core-mantle grains, carbonaceous particles and PAH-like molecules.

2 When the dust enters a dense gas cloud, atoms and molecules of gas adhere to the core-mantle grains and form an outer mantle of ice. The carbonaceous particles and PAH-like molecules also accrete on the core-mantle grains.

3 Ultraviolet radiation processes the material in the ice mantle, creating a layer of complex organic compounds ("yellow stuff").

4 As the cloud contracts to form a star, some of the core-mantle grains clump together and become comet nuclei. But the vast majority of the dust is dispersed.

5 Returning to a diffuse cloud, the core-mantle grain is exposed to harsher radiation that evaporates the ice mantle and further processes the organic material. The "yellow stuff" turns brown.

6 Supernova shock fronts accelerate the grains, causing violent collisions that shatter the organic mantles. The debris becomes the carbonaceous particles and PAH-like molecules.

University of Wisconsin–Madison has hypothesized that the larger grains are porous aggregates of small graphite and silicate particles. But these models cannot adequately explain another effect of interstellar dust: how it polarizes the light passing through it, orienting the electromagnetic waves in a particular direction. To account for this phenomenon, we know that each of the larger dust grains must be shaped roughly like a cylinder or a spheroid and spin around its shorter axis like a twirling baton. Furthermore, we know that the spin axes of all the dust grains must be pointing in the same direction to polarize the light. (Magnetic fields in the dust cloud are believed to align the spin axes.) The unique achievement of the unified dust model is that the hypothesized core-mantle particles can account for the observed polarization at all wavelengths.

From Dust to Comets

Comets are believed to be the most pristine relics of the protosolar nebula—the cloud of gas and dust that gave birth to our own solar system. As astronomers make new discoveries about the chemical composition of both comets and interstellar dust, they are becoming convinced that comets originally formed as clumps of dust grains. It therefore stands to reason that comet observations will tell us more about the dust.

When the planets and comets were born along with the sun about 4.6 billion years ago, the core-mantle dust grains in the protosolar cloud had most likely absorbed all the smaller carbonaceous particles and PAH-like molecules, as well as all the carbon monoxide and other volatiles in the gas. Only the hydrogen and helium remained free. The dust grains collided with one another frequently enough to form large, loosely clumped aggregates. The prevailing theory is that these "fluffy" clusters of interstellar dust particles evolved into the nuclei of the comets. Each nucleus would be very porous—that is, it would contain a lot of empty space. My own model of a piece of a comet nucleus contains 100 average-size protosolar dust grains jumbled together in a three-micron-wide aggregate, in which 80 percent of the volume is empty space.

Since their birth, the comets have been orbiting the sun in the regions of the Oort Cloud and the Kuiper Belt at distances far beyond the orbits of the planets. Occasionally, though, gravitational disturbances kick comets into orbits that take them closer to the sun. A revolution in our understanding of comets occurred in 1986, when the space probes Giotto and Vega 1 and 2 flew by Comet Halley, which approaches the sun every 76 years. All three spacecraft carried spectrometers for measuring the mass and chemical composition of the particles from Halley's coma, the cloud of gas and dust surrounding the nucleus. The dust particles hit the detectors at 80 kilometers per second and broke up into their atomic components. The instruments detected a wide range of particle masses, including the 10^{-14} gram expected for individual core-mantle dust grains and the 10^{-18} gram typical of smaller carbonaceous particles.

Jochen Kissel of the Max Planck Institute for Extraterrestrial Physics in Garching, Germany, Franz R. Krueger of the Krueger Inigenieurburo in Darmstadt and Elmar K. Jessburger of the University of Münster later confirmed that the dust from Halley consists of aggregates of particles with silicate cores and organic refractory mantles—just as my origin theory for comets predicts. Their conclusion was based on the fact that the oxygen, carbon and nitrogen atoms from the organic mantles hit the spacecraft's detectors just before the silicon, magnesium and iron atoms from the cores did.

How old is the dust contained in Halley and the other comets? We know that when the dust clumped together to form the comets it was already about five billion years old, because a typical dust grain remains in interstellar space for about that long before it is consumed in star formation. And because the comets are themselves 4.6 billion years old, the dust probably dates back to nearly 10 billion years ago. Analyzing comet material therefore allows us to probe the infancy of the Milky Way.

Comet dust may also have played a role in seeding life on Earth. Each loose cluster of comet dust not only contains organic materials but also has a structure that is ideal for chemical evolution once it is immersed in water. Kissel and Krueger have shown that small molecules could easily penetrate the clump from the outside, but large molecules would remain stuck inside. Such a structure could stimulate the production of ever larger and more complex molecules, possibly serving as a tiny incubator for the first primitive life-forms. A single comet could have deposited up to 10^{25} of these "seeds" on the young Earth.

The National Aeronautics and Space Administration and the European Space Agency (ESA) are undertaking missions that will reveal more about the nature of comets and interstellar dust. NASA's Stardust craft, launched last year, is scheduled to rendezvous with Comet Wild-2 in 2004 and bring back a sample of the dust from that comet's coma. While in transit, the probe is also collecting samples of the interstellar dust streaming through our solar system. The ESA's Rosetta mission is even more ambitious. Scheduled for launch in 2003, the craft will go into orbit around the nucleus of Comet Wirtanen and send a probe to land on the surface of the porous body. An array of scientific instruments on the lander will thoroughly analyze the comet's physical structure and chemical composition. My research group will participate in the effort by preparing laboratory samples of organic materials for comparison with those observed in Wirtanen's nucleus and dust.

These space missions will no doubt open new paths for research. Astronomers no longer consider interstellar dust a nuisance. Rather it is a major source of information about the birth of stars, planets and comets, and it may even hold clues to the origin of life itself.

Further Information

The Structure and Evolution of Interstellar Grains.
J. Mayo Greenberg in *Scientific American*, Vol.
250, No. 6, pages 124–135; June 1984.

A Unified Model of Interstellar Dust. Aigen Li and
J. Mayo Greenberg in *Astronomy and Astrophysics*,
Vol. 323, No. 2, pages 566–584; 1997.

Cosmic Dust in the 21st Century. J. Mayo Greenberg
and Chuanjian Shen in Astrophysics and Space
Science, Vol. 269–270/1–4, pages 33–55; 1999.
The article is available at http://arXiv.org/abs/
astro-ph/0006337 on the World Wide Web.

About The Author

J. MAYO GREENBERG received his Ph.D. in
theoretical physics from Johns Hopkins University in
1948. In 1975 he came to the University of Leiden
in the Netherlands to establish and direct its Laboratory
for Astrophysics, where he has studied the chemical
evolution of interstellar dust, the composition of
comets and the origin of life.

"Galaxies behind
7. the Milky Way"

by Renée C. Kraan-Korteweg and Ofer Lahav

Over a fifth of the universe is hidden from view, blocked by dust and stars in the disk of our galaxy. But over the past few years, astronomers have found ways to peek through the murk.

On a dark night, far from city lights, we can clearly see the disk of our galaxy shimmering as a broad band across the sky. This diffuse glow is the direct light emitted by hundreds of billions of stars as well as the indirect starlight scattered by dust grains in interstellar space. We are located about 28,000 light-years from the center of the galaxy in the midst of this disk. But although the Milky Way may be a glorious sight, it is a constant source of frustration for astronomers who study the universe beyond our galaxy. The disk blocks light from a full 20 percent of the cosmos, and it seems to be a very exciting 20 percent.

Somewhere behind the disk, for example, are crucial parts of the two biggest structures in the nearby universe: the Perseus-Pisces supercluster of galaxies and the "Great Attractor," a gargantuan agglomeration of matter whose existence has been inferred from the motions of thousands of galaxies through space. Observations also show a tantalizing number of bright and nearby galaxies in the general direction of the disk, suggesting there are many others that go unseen. Without knowing what lies in our blind spot, researchers

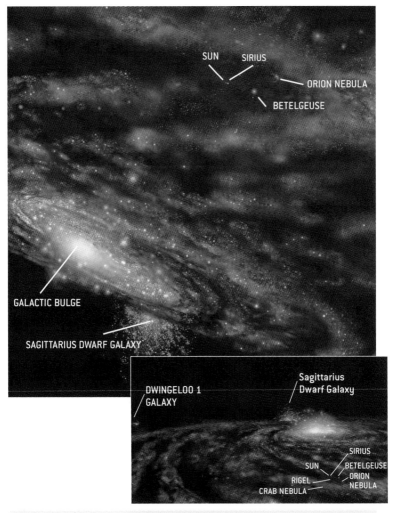

Disk of Milky Way galaxy, a cosmic crepe with one trillion suns' worth of stars, dust and gas, prevents us from viewing a fifth of the universe. Among the hidden objects is the Sagittarius dwarf spheroidal galaxy, apparent in these artist's impressions of the view from below (*main illustration*) and above (*inset*) the plane of the Milky Way. Our sight lines to the dwarf are almost completely blocked by the bulge of stars surrounding the center of our galaxy. Although Sagittarius is the closest galaxy to our own, it was only discovered in 1994. Another hidden galaxy, Dwingeloo 1, is shown in the inset.

cannot fully map the matter in our corner of the cosmos. This in turn prevents them from settling some of the most important questions in cosmology: How large are cosmic structures? How did they form? What is the total density of matter in the universe?

Only in recent years have astronomers developed the techniques to peer through the disk and to reconstruct the veiled universe from its effects on those parts that can be seen. Although observers are far from completing this tedious task, some spectacular discoveries have already proved that it is worth the effort. Among other things, astronomers have found a new galaxy so close that it would dominate our skies were it not obscured by the disk. They have found colossal galaxy clusters never before seen and have even taken a first peek at the core of the elusive Great Attractor.

The obscuration of galaxies by the Milky Way was first perceived when astronomers began distinguishing external galaxies from internal nebulae, both seen simply as faint, extended objects. Because galaxies appeared everywhere except in the region of the Milky Way, this region was named the "zone of avoidance" [see "Three-Dimensional View" box]. Scientists now know that external galaxies consist of billions of stars as well as countless clouds of dust and gas. In the zone of avoidance the light of the galaxies is usually swamped by the huge number of foreground stars or is absorbed by the dust in our own galaxy.

Extragalactic astronomers have generally avoided this zone, too, concentrating instead on unobscured regions of the sky. But 20 years ago a crucial observation hinted at what they might be missing. Crude measurements of the cosmic microwave background radiation, a relic of the big bang, showed a 180-degree asymmetry, known as a dipole. It is about 0.1 percent hotter than average at one location in the sky and equally colder in the catercornered site. These measurements, confirmed by the Cosmic Background Explorer satellite in 1989 and 1990, suggest that our galaxy and its neighbors, the so-called Local Group, are moving at 600 kilometers per second (1.34 million miles per hour) in the direction of the constellation Hydra. This vector is derived after correcting for known motions, such as the revolution of the sun around the galactic center and the motion of our galaxy toward its neighbor spiral galaxy, Andromeda.

Where does this motion, which is a small deviation from the otherwise uniform expansion of the universe, come from? Galaxies are clumped into groups and clusters, and these themselves agglomerate into superclusters, leaving other regions devoid of galaxies. The clumpy mass distribution surrounding the Local Group may exert an unbalanced gravitational attraction, pulling it in one direction. At first glance, it might seem hard to believe that galaxies could influence one another over the vast distances that separate them. But relative to their masses, galaxies are closer to one another than individual stars within our galaxy are.

The expected velocity of the Local Group can be calculated by adding up the gravitational forces caused by known galaxies. Although the resulting vector is

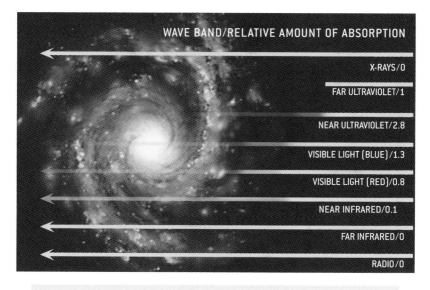

WAVE BAND/RELATIVE AMOUNT OF ABSORPTION

X-RAYS / 0

FAR ULTRAVIOLET / 1

NEAR ULTRAVIOLET / 2.8

VISIBLE LIGHT (BLUE) / 1.3

VISIBLE LIGHT (RED) / 0.8

NEAR INFRARED / 0.1

FAR INFRARED / 0

RADIO / 0

Light from other galaxies penetrates the Milky Way to varying degrees, depending on its wavelength. The longest wavelengths, which correspond to radio and far-infrared radiation, are hardly affected, but shorter wavelengths (such as near-infrared, visible and ultraviolet light) are blocked by the dust and gas clouds within our galaxy. For very short wavelengths, such as the most powerful x-rays, the gas becomes transparent again.

within 20 degrees of the observed cosmic background dipole, the calculations remain highly uncertain, partly because they do not take into account the galaxies behind the zone of avoidance.

The lingering discrepancy between the dipole direction and the expected velocity vector has led astronomers to postulate "attractors." One research group, later referred to as the Seven Samurai, used the motions of hundreds of galaxies to deduce the existence of the Great Attractor about 200 million light-years away [see "The Large-Scale Streaming of Galaxies," by Alan Dressler; *Scientific American*, September 1987]. The Local Group seems to be caught in a cosmic tug of war between the Great Attractor and the equally distant Perseus-Pisces supercluster, which is on the opposite side of the sky. To know which will win the war, astronomers need to know the mass of the hidden parts of these structures.

Both are components of a long chain of galaxies known as the Supergalactic Plane. The formation of such a megastructure is thought to depend on the nature of the invisible dark matter that makes up the bulk of the universe. Chains of galaxies should be more likely in a universe dominated by particles of so-called hot dark matter (such as massive neutrinos) rather than by cold dark matter (such as axions or other hypothetical particles). But astronomers cannot distinguish between these two possibilities until they map the structures fully.

Nearby galaxies are not to be ignored in the bulk motion of the Local Group. Because gravity is strongest at small distances, a significant force is generated by the nearest galaxies, even if they are not massive. And it is intriguing that five of the eight apparently brightest galaxies lie in the zone of avoidance; they are so close and bright that they shine through the murk. These galaxies belong to the galaxy groups Centaurus A and IC342, close neighbors to our Local Group. For each member of these groups that astronomers manage to see, there are probably many others whose light is entirely blocked.

Lifting the Fog

Our vantage point, to be sure, could be worse. If we lived in the nearby Andromeda galaxy, the obscured part of the sky would not be much different, yet we would also lose our clear view of the nearest galaxy cluster in Virgo. But even a habitual optimist would admit that we are somewhat unlucky. Because the orbit of the sun about the galactic center is inclined to the galactic plane, the solar system partakes in an epicyclic motion above and below the plane. Currently we are elevated only 40 light-years from the plane. If we had been born 15 million years from now, we would be located nearly 300 light-years above the plane—beyond the thickest layer of obscuration—and could view one side of the current zone of avoidance. It will take another 35 million years to cross the disk of the Milky Way to the other side.

Most astronomers do not want to wait that long to learn about the extragalactic sky behind the zone of avoidance. What can they do in the meantime? A first step is careful review of existing visible-light images. The dust in the zone does not completely blot out every galaxy; some poke through, although they seem dimmer and smaller the closer they are to the middle of the galactic plane. The odd appearance of these galaxies, in combination with the high density of foreground stars, can confuse the computer software used to analyze images and recognize galaxies. So various groups of astronomers have gone back to the old-fashioned way of examining images—by eye. Photographic plates from the Palomar Observatory sky survey and its Southern Hemisphere counterpart, conducted in the 1950s, have been painstakingly searched over the past 10 years. Researchers have covered a major fraction of the zone of avoidance, identifying 50,000 previously uncatalogued galaxies.

In areas where the extinction of light by dust is too severe, however, galaxies are fully obscured, and other methods are required. The leading option is to observe at longer wavelengths; the longer the wavelength, the less the radiation interacts with microscopic dust particles. The 21-centimeter spectral line emitted by electrically neutral hydrogen gas is ideal in this respect. It traces gas-rich spiral galaxies, intrinsically dim galaxies and dwarf galaxies—that is, most galaxies except gas-poor elliptical galaxies.

In 1987 a pioneering 21-centimeter project was launched by Patricia A. Henning of the University of New Mexico and Frank J. Kerr of the University of Maryland. They pointed the 91-meter radio telescope at Green Bank, W.Va., toward random spots in the zone of avoidance and detected 18 previously unknown galaxies. Unfortunately, the telescope collapsed spectacularly before they could finish their project. (Its replacement is due to be completed next year.) A more systematic survey was initiated by an international team that includes us. Conducted at the 25-meter Dwingeloo radio telescope in the Netherlands, this longer-term project is mapping all the spiral galaxies in the northern part of the zone of avoidance out to a distance of 175 million light-years. So far it has discovered 40 galaxies.

Last year another international collaboration, led by Lister Staveley-Smith of the Australia Telescope National Facility in Marsfield and one of us (Kraan-Korteweg), began an even more sensitive survey of the southern Milky Way. This survey, which maps galaxies out to 500 million light-years, uses a custom-built instrument at the 64-meter radio telescope at Parkes, Australia. More than 100 galaxies have already been detected, and thousands more are expected when the survey reaches its full depth.

The radio-wave bands are not the only possible peepholes through the zone of avoidance. Infrared light, too, is less affected by dust than visible light is. In the early 1980s the Infrared Astronomical Satellite (IRAS) surveyed the whole sky in far-infrared wave-lengths (those closer to radio wavelengths). It tentatively identified infrared-bright galaxies, particularly spirals and starburst galaxies, in which stars are forming rapidly and plentifully. IRAS-selected galaxy candidates near the zone of avoidance are now being reexamined with images taken in the near-infrared wavelengths (those closer to visible light).

Two systematic near-infrared surveys, due to be finished in 2000, are also under way: the Two Micron All-Sky Survey, an American project, and DENIS, a European project that focuses on the Southern Hemisphere. Both surveys take digital images in three wave bands that probe the older stellar population in galaxies. The surveys easily trace the elliptical galaxies found at the center of dense galaxy concentrations; they therefore complement the far-infrared and 21-centimeter bands, which predominantly find spiral galaxies. A pilot study has shown that the near-infrared surveys do indeed uncover galaxies that fail to register on visible-light photographs. Unfortunately, neither visible nor infrared light can pick out galaxies in the thickest parts of the galactic plane.

Another possible way to overcome the obscuration is to observe at very short wavelengths, such as x-rays. Highly populated galaxy clusters emit copious x-rays, which pass through the Milky Way almost unhindered. But an x-ray investigation, which could draw on existing data from ROSAT and other satellites, has not been done yet.

In addition to direct observations, astronomers are exploring the zone of avoidance by indirect means. Signal-processing techniques, commonly applied by engineers to noisy and incomplete data, have been used successfully by researchers at the Hebrew University and one of us (Lahav) to predict the existence of clusters such as Puppis and Vela, as well as the continuity of the Supergalactic Plane across the zone. The galaxy velocities can also be used on both sides of the zone to predict the mass distribution in between. With this method the center of the Great Attractor was predicted to lie on a line connecting the constellations Centaurus and Pavo. These reconstruction methods, however, deduce only the largest-scale features across the zone; they miss individual galaxies and smaller clusters.

Prey of the Milky Way

Such methods are slowly opening up the hidden fifth of the universe to astronomical investigation. A most surprising discovery came in 1994, when Rodrigo A. Ibata, then at the University of British Columbia, Gerard F. Gilmore of the University of Cambridge and Michael J. Irwin of the Royal Greenwich Observatory in Cambridge, England, who were studying stars in our Milky Way, accidentally found a galaxy right on our doorstep. Named the Sagittarius dwarf, it is now the closest known galaxy—just 80,000 light-years away from the solar system, less than half the distance of the next closest, the Large Magellanic Cloud. In fact, it is located well inside our galaxy, on the far side of the galactic center.

Because the Sagittarius dwarf lies directly behind the central bulge of the Milky Way, it cannot be seen in direct images. Its serendipitous detection was based on velocity measurements of stars: the researchers spotted a set of stars moving differently from those in our galaxy. By pinpointing the stars with this velocity, looking for others at the same distance and compensating for the light of known foreground stars, they mapped out the dwarf. It extends at least 20 degrees from end to end, making it the largest apparent structure in the sky after the Milky Way itself. Its angular size corresponds to a diameter of at least 28,000 light-years, about a fifth of the size of our galaxy, even though the dwarf is only a thousandth as massive.

Many popular models of galaxy formation postulate that large galaxies are formed by a long process of aggregation of many smaller galaxies. Such a process should still be common today, yet has been observed only rarely. Sagittarius appears to have undergone some disruption from the tidal forces exerted by the Milky Way, but the disruption of the core of Sagittarius is unexpectedly minor. The dwarf may have orbited our galaxy 10 times or more yet remains largely intact, indicating that it is held together by large amounts of dark matter (as opposed to luminous matter such as stars or gaseous clouds). Even so, its demise is just a matter of time; some studies suggest that Sagittarius may have only another billion years to go before being swallowed by our galaxy. Its discovery has demonstrated that mergers do happen, that they happen today and that they do not necessarily wreck the disk of the larger galaxy.

Sagittarius is one of many surprises to have surfaced from the zone of avoidance. In August 1994 we and the rest of the Dwingeloo Obscured Galaxy Survey team examined our first 21-centimeter spectra. We selected a region where many filaments are lost in the zone and where the nearby galaxy group IC342 resides. Quite soon we came across an intriguing radio spectrum in the direction of the constellation Cassiopeia. Radio observations are prone to interference, which can mimic extragalactic radio profiles; moreover, the feature blended with the emission from galactic gas. Yet various tests confirmed the signal, marking the discovery of another previously unknown nearby galaxy.

George K. T. Hau of the University of Cambridge identified an extremely dim visible-light object that matched the location of this radio signal. Before long, deeper images were obtained at various telescopes, which fully revealed the shape of the galaxy: a bar with spiral arms protruding at its ends. If it were not lying behind the plane of the Milky Way, the galaxy—named Dwingeloo 1—would be one of the 10 brightest in the sky. Judging from its rate of rotation it has about one third the mass of the Milky Way, making it comparable to M33, the third heaviest galaxy of the Local Group after the Milky Way and Andromeda.

While conducting follow-up observations of Dwingeloo 1, the Westerbork Synthesis Radio Telescope in the Netherlands discovered a second galaxy just one third of a degree away: Dwingeloo 2, a dwarf galaxy with half the diameter and a tenth of the mass of Dwingeloo 1. Located at a distance of 10 million light-years, the pair of galaxies is close to, but just beyond, the Local Group. They seem to be associated with IC342. Two other galaxies in this assemblage were later discovered on sensitive optical images.

Although astronomers have yet to explore the entire zone of avoidance, they can now rule out other Andromeda-size galaxies in our backyard. The Milky

Way and Andromeda are indeed the dominant galaxies of the Local Group. Disappointing though the lack of another major discovery may be, it removes the uncertainties in the kinematics of our immediate neighborhood.

Clusters and Superclusters

Studies in the zone of avoidance have also upset astronomers' ideas of the more distant universe. Using the 100-meter radio telescope near Effelsberg, Germany, astronomers discovered a new cluster 65 million light-years away in the constellation Puppis. Several other lines of evidence, including an analysis of galaxies discovered by IRAS, have converged on the same conclusion: the inclusion of Puppis brings the expected motion of the Local Group into better agreement with the observed cosmic background dipole.

Could these searches demystify the Great Attractor? Although the density of visible galaxies does increase in the attractor's presumed direction, the core of this amorphous mass has eluded researchers. A cluster was identified in roughly the right location by George O. Abell in the 1980s, at which time it was the only known cluster in the zone of avoidance. But with a mere 50 galaxies, it could hardly amount to an attractor, let alone a great one.

The true richness and significance of this cluster has become clear in the recent searches. Kraan-Korteweg, with Patrick A. Woudt of the European Southern Observatories in Garching, Germany, has discovered another 600 galaxies in the cluster. With colleagues in France and South Africa, we obtained spectral observations at various telescopes in the Southern Hemisphere. The observed velocities of the galaxies suggest that the cluster is very massive indeed—on par with the well-known Coma cluster, an agglomeration 10,000 times as massive as our galaxy. At long last, astronomers have seen the center of the Great Attractor. Along with surrounding clusters, this discovery could fully explain the observed galaxy motions in the nearby universe.

The hierarchy of cosmic structure does not end there. Searches in the zone of avoidance have identified still larger clumpings. One supercluster 370 million light-years away in the constellation Ophiuchus was identified by Kenichi Wakamatsu of Gifu University in Japan. Although this supercluster lies behind the galactic center, a region extremely crowded with stars, Wakamatsu identified thousands of its galaxies on sky-survey plates. The Ophiuchus supercluster might be connected to another supercluster in the constellation Hercules, suggesting coherent structures on scales that are mind-boggling even to astronomers.

For generations of astronomers, the zone of avoidance has been an obstacle in investigating fundamental issues such as the formation of the Milky Way, the origin of the Local Group motion, the connectivity of chains of galaxies and the true

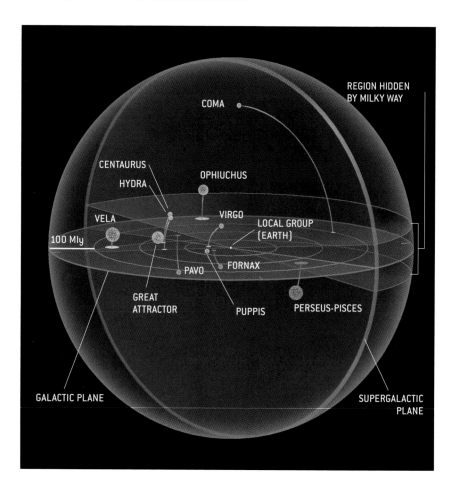

REGION HIDDEN
BY MILKY WAY

COMA

CENTAURUS
HYDRA
OPHIUCHUS

VELA
VIRGO
LOCAL GROUP
(EARTH)

100 Mly

PAVO
FORNAX

GREAT
ATTRACTOR
PUPPIS
PERSEUS-PISCES

GALACTIC PLANE
SUPERGALACTIC
PLANE

Three-dimensional view of the local universe reveals the uneven distribution of galaxy clusters. The outermost sphere represents a distance of 400 million light-years (Mly) from the Milky Way, the horizontal plane is the galactic plane extended into intergalactic space, the small knots of dots are galaxy clusters, and the circles are their projections onto the galactic plane. Many galaxy clusters lie on or near the Supergalactic Plane. Some are hidden in the zone of avoidance (*region hidden by Milky Way*).

number of galaxies in the universe. The efforts over the past decade to lift this thick screen have turned the former zone of avoidance into one of the most exciting regions in the extragalactic sky. The mysterious Great Attractor is now well mapped; the discovery of the Sagittarius dwarf has shown how the Milky Way formed; and the vast cosmic filaments challenge theories of dark matter and structure formation. More surprises in this *caelum incognitum* may await astronomers. Step by step, the missing pieces of the extragalactic sky are being filled in.

Further Reading

Principles of Physical Cosmology. P.J.E. Peebles. Princeton University Press, 1993.

Unveiling Large-Scale Structures behind the Milky Way. Edited by Chantal Balkowski and R. C. Kraan-Korteweg. Astronomical Society of the Pacific Conference Series, Vol. 67; January 1994.

A Dwarf Satellite Galaxy in Sagittarius. R. A. Ibata, G. Gilmore and M. J. Irwin in *Nature*, Vol. 370, pages 194–196; July 21, 1994.

Dynamics of Cosmic Flows. Avishai Dekel in *Annual Review of Astronomy and Astrophysics*, Vol. 32, pages 371–418; 1994.

A Nearby Massive Cluster behind the Milky Way. R. C. Kraan-Korteweg et al. in *Nature*, Vol. 379, pages 519–521; February 8, 1996.

About The Authors

RENÉE C. KRAAN-KORTEWEG and *OFER LAHAV* joined forces in 1990, after they met in Durham, England, at a conference on cosmology; independently, they both had discovered a previously unknown cluster behind the Milky Way in the constellation Puppis. Kraan-Korteweg is a professor in the department of astronomy of the University of Guanajuato in Mexico. Lahav is a faculty member of the Institute of Astronomy at the University of Cambridge and a Fellow of St. Catharine's College. Kraan-Korteweg explores the zone of avoidance by direct observation, whereas Lahav utilizes theoretical and computational techniques.

Web Sites

Due to the changing nature of Internet links, Rosen Publishing has developed an online list of Web sites related to the subject of this book. This site is updated regularly. Please use this link to access the list:

http://www.rosenlinks.com/saces/miwa

For Further Reading

Belkora, Leila. *Minding the Heavens: The Story of Our Discovery of the Milky Way*. Oxford, England: Taylor & Francis, 2002.

Greene, Brian. *The Fabric of the Cosmos: Space, Time, and the Texture of Reality*. New York, NY: Vintage, 2005.

Kidger, Mark. *Astronomical Enigmas: Life on Mars, the Star of Bethlehem, and Other Milky Way Mysteries*. Baltimore, MD: The Johns Hopkins University Press, 2005.

Skurzynski, Gloria. *Are We Alone? Scientists Search for Life in Space*. Washington, DC: National Geographic Children's Books, 2004.

Tyson, Neil deGrasse. *Death by Black Hole: And Other Cosmic Quandaries*. New York, NY: W. W. Norton, 2007.

Index